CONQUERING CORPORATE ENEMIES

ENEMIES

MIND · PERSONALITIES · SITUATIONS

YVETTE C. OWENS

Legal Disclaimer

Connect with MPowered Voice Publishing
www.MPoweredvoicepublishing.ca

Table of Contents

Contents

FOREWORD

When Yvette Owens invited me to write the foreword for her *Conquering Corporate Enemies* book, I quickly accepted the honor. The invitation honored me because this is a book of absolute importance by an author with experiential ability to speak to this great challenge in the corporate world. It has been a treat for me to read the manuscript, experiencing the heart behind the words that have been so carefully and thoughtfully written by the author. Yvette Owens is a professional who is greatly respected by all who know her and her work.

I hope that, with this book, she will receive the acclaim that her thoughts and writing have, for so long, deserved. It will bring about change and liberation to every reader.

It would be an understatement to say that conquering corporate enemies is an important topic. The words, actions, attitudes, experiences, and beliefs of every person in the world produce an effect on someone. Each of us, we endeavor to live with integrity by always leading with the character that, no matter what, your position shapes the surrounding environments. I can imagine, at times, on her journey, Yvette considered that taking such a subject to address would be an exercise in futility if it would not prepare us to confront and survive many of the circumstances described in the book. I applaud her courage and persistence to release this much needed conversation with many areas of culture, including corporate. I invite you to read Yvette Owen's *Conquering Corporate Enemies*. You will find not only great insight but all the elements and essential information necessary to become a change agent in your immediate atmosphere of life.

Beverley M. Vaughn

Introduction

My colleague and long-time friend, Maria, called out from behind me, "So, is that what answered prayer looks like?" She was referencing the scene she just witnessed as I embraced one of my greatest nemeses, a leader from my past who, daily, looked for ways to tear me down and make me believe I was not good enough. Every meeting and even casual conversation attempted to make me question my validity in the role I held at that time. Hallelujah, it was for my good. I am bold and courageous to know and stand for who I am and what I bring to the table despite what anyone says or thinks. Self-confidence, not arrogance, was resurrected after years of working in environments where others attempted to make me dependent on them for my success or simply used me for their gain.

Yes, what my dear friend witnessed was the answer to many prayers. Maria heard many of the incidents and unfair treatment I experienced at the hand of this individual. Prayer provided strength for me to get through tough times and gave me the ability to pray for my enemies. Now, I genuinely know how prayer can change my enemy and me so we could, at the very least, be able to greet each other with a smile and a hug. I remember a time when only God could cause me to be by her and her family's side when tragedy hit. Driving the long-distance, several towns from my home, during my vacation, to the funeral services, I did not want to run into others of her circle from work. I pondered, 'Why do I feel as though I need to attend this service?' I arrived to find that no other member of our organization attended. Not even those who appeared to be extremely close to her. I supposed they must have all participated in the wake the night before. I found myself hoping that this was the case. How sad, I thought for her, to so vehemently support leaders and, then, not to have their support during a very personal time of loss. Here I was prompted to walk in love, even when it did not make sense to the human flesh. God knows why and therefore helped me carry out that assignment.

"This is no afternoon athletic contest that we'll walk away from and forget about in a couple of hours. This is for keeps, a life-or-death fight to the finish against the Devil and all his angels." Ephesians 6:12 (The Message)

What this book is not

This book is not a generalization of all corporate organizations because evil attacks are very personalized. They come after targeted individuals for specific purposes to stop the progression of success towards destiny. The intent is not racial bashing. I am not taking a stand against gentrification *(the process of renewing and rebuilding to accompany the influx of middle-class or affluent people into deteriorating areas that often displaces poorer residents),* or age group glorification. The identity of the individuals in each scenario recounted in this book is not significant. The names are changed to protect the innocent and the guilty. The truth is any of us if we allow it to satisfy our desires, conscious or unconscious, can be influenced by evil forces on any given day.

The power comes when we recognize that there genuinely are both good and evil forces at work in this world. Both energies show up in individuals. For example, at times, we are targeted for love. God is love. While at other times, we are infiltrated with thoughts to distract, discourage, and destroy us. Those thoughts come from evil forces, our enemy. The truth is that we have to recognize the difference and, then, choose to whom we will listen and respond, at any given time. If we are not careful, the subtlety of the enemy's encroachment can often take us unaware. After the fact, we become disappointed in our behavior once we see the impact. At the same time, God is continuously available to those who wish to trust and rely on His excellent guidance and judgment.

The bottom line, it is all about choice and conduct. Choose every day whom you will respond to, and your behavior will follow your choice. It can be a real struggle when you desire to get in the mix. Real strength is required to conquer the enemy and your desire, which is contrary to the love God calls us to release and walk-in.

"There is a way that seems right to a man and appears straight before him, but at the end of it is the way of death." Proverbs 16:25 (AMPC)

What this book is

This book reflects my corporate experiences, from what I have observed happening to others and the difficult times through which I helped mentees, family, and friends. Corporate is not limited to just large organizations. It has everything to do with any environment where people come together to complete a set of objectives, from fortune five hundred companies to church organizations to college campuses, to name a few. I intend to fully expose situations, personalities, and mindsets that so many have endured to give the reader insight into what it feels like when exposed to those behaviors. I will also share the shift in mindset, personality, and (in some cases) situations that helped to overcome what felt impossible at the time.

Perhaps some can relate to my walk of nearly 40 years and find solace in knowing that they were not alone as they may have gone through similar situations. Others may find this helpful as they venture into the corporate arenas. Finally, I hope some readers will make better choices as they lead. Enhance your effectiveness and strengthen your organization by valuing the diversity of thought and persons, having respect for each individual, and aiming to utilize each person's gifts while providing targeted development that satisfies the needs of the organization and the individual. The majority of people take pride in bringing their best to an organization. An organization that under-utilizes individuals or attempts to degrade their team ends up with far less than the combined potential of the organization. Likewise, any organization that settles for using and draining any individual will not have sustained quality growth. No one is hanging around, waiting to be used and abused, especially once they get a sense of what is happening.

I appreciate the knowledge that I gained and the individuals I encountered throughout the years. We are all unique characters with the good, the bad, and the ugly. Choice and conduct rule the day. Coming into the mega-corporate business world, I had no prior experience or preparation by way of fireside chats with any family member who was CEO, CFO, or COO. What I knew about business, I learned in college and churches. I have a natural proclivity towards business. I did not have anyone in the workplace 'covering' me as so many do. I can genuinely say the grace of God kept me. He promoted and built storyline is released now. I am at peace with my identity and confidence intact.

Of course, no man is an island. Yes, I have had help along the way, some of which was undercover. Others expressed that they were not sure why they were helping me, but just knew that they needed to help. It is so strange that my biggest supporters and encouragers have been my peers and members of the teams I have led. I had leaders wanting to help, but the risk was too high. Some peers advanced because their leaders were in a more position than those leading. The person who has the ear of the decision-makers is critical. Those in representing teams should lead with their heart and not what is convenient for them. In each group, some individuals have a significant influence on known and (sometimes) unknown reasons. The input of these persons can influence your growth opportunities or do just the opposite, regardless of reporting relationships. If they are influential and speak on your behalf, it is excellent. If they are prominent and they share concerns with your performance even in the smallest way, it may not matter what positive thing your leader says about you. The favorite in the room has spoken, and their voice carries far more weight than the one who has witnessed your performance.

I hope that readers will see and understand the unhealthy cultures and behaviors that seem harmless but, at the very core, are detrimental. I hope that this book encourages an influx of integrity, compassion, and innovative strategies and tactics that empower every member of any organization to not only understand their role and responsibilities but also to know they are truly valued and rewarded in the organization.

'Conquering Corporate Enemies Mind, Personalities, Situations' is the memoir of a black woman of faith, born in 1960 in Baltimore, Maryland, USA, who relocated to Southern New Jersey, the USA, in her sophomore year of high school. I transitioned from a predominately black school system to mostly white institutions, a high school in New Jersey, College in New Hampshire, and MBA in Connecticut. There were five black students in each graduating class. I have been in church, working in multiple capacities all my life. I lived through the race riots in Baltimore after the assassination of Rev. Dr. Martin Luther King Jr. I was receiving threatening letters in my locker in high school and my hotel room as I traveled with the school band – all while trying to get an education. Yet God always placed loving and kind white people in my life who genuinely cared for and about me. Like the Dean of Student Affairs in NH, who went out of his way every Sunday to travel 20 miles one way to pick me up, take me to church with his family, invite me to have lunch and dinner with his family, and then bring me back to campus. God did not allow me to have a bitter heart. Even in the workplace, there were members of my team who spoke out against injustices towards me that they experienced firsthand.

The root causes of injustices, unfair treatment, rude behavior, and the like are demonic forces. They come to cause division, prevent progress, to kill, steal, and destroy. They will use whatever they can to bring you down. Be wise. See what is really behind the behavior and learn how to fight and stand firm. I stood by the grace of God for nearly 40 years in the corporate workplace and church. I have never been without a job, and I have had continued success. I have been led to five different churches, primarily due to relocation until a switch was necessary, most recently, for spiritual freedom, growth, and maturity. At the same time, I lead a community organization in my town, county, and state. This summary is the fabric of who I am. God has kept me through it all, and I am so incredibly grateful. My prayer is that you will open your hearts and minds to my truth as you experience my journey toward purpose.

God bless every one of you, abundantly.

Yvette C. Owens

Satan's Hound Dogs

I hear dogs barking—vicious barks from a pack of dogs that are tight on my heels, ready to attack me. Growling in anger with sharp white fangs positioned to bite when the opportunity presents itself. Intimidation straight from the enemy's camp, as if it is not enough that I report to a witches' cove. A significant dose of morning devotions full of prayer, songs of worship and praise, and declarations are the only way to start my day. I reinforce my peace and strength this way just to maintain my sanity.

I need strength to keep going, especially when others look like me, trying to convince me that I just need to relax and not have my guard up. Each time I heard this suggestion, my thoughts were, *'Excuse me, I am under attack! The struggle is real for me.'* Others watch to see how I handle the adversity as a Christian believer in the workplace. Will I maintain my peace and still walk in love? How do you do that and keep the hound dogs from getting to your juggler's vein? How do I walk in love when the witches have conspired to discredit me? They plant doubt in the minds of my team while attempting to mess with my psyche via blatant one on one conversations, professing what I am not and what skills or talents I do not have.

The struggle is genuine, the death howl draws close, and I am to relax? My response, *'You are the one to be in the clan for whatever reason, legitimate or not. You are in and held close. Is it to make it more difficult for anyone to claim discrimination? The enemy is conniving and fierce. Even if your position and status among the leaders are positive and legit, which it very well could be, that does not make my experience any less legit.'*

After nearly 40 years of growth, respect, and successful experiences working with a multitude of leaders, I now recognize that I have reached a turning point, a pinnacle in my working career that I must fight through because the dogs are coming towards me. I am entering and expecting to go to the Vice President officer level, and all hell is against me. Let us be clear. My writing is not a case of reaching the end of my skills and talents. I am not arrogant or prideful. I work hard, confirmed by decades of favorable performance reviews and bonuses. I take stretch assignments and offer strategic and tactical suggestions to strengthen the organization and its people in my sphere of influence.

The witches are brewing, and the human resources department acknowledges it, off the record, of course. My direct leader informed me that comments about me, made supposedly by him, were taken out of context. Yet, your recommendation for me is to relax and not be combative? I felt like I was fighting for my life. Leave? Where to? Why allow them to win and take years of pension and retirement benefits away from me that I would not get back at this point in my career? Sure, it is easy to run. It may appear to be easier to start over somewhere else, but that is not my lot. I am to ride this out in the grace that is within. Why? So I can share with others who have gone or are going through similar situations. I intend to let them know that they were not crazy when others said they imagined the attacks or that they must have done something to warrant it. I hope to bring comfort in acknowledging that if it happened to me and others sited in this book, then what you experienced could very well have been real, too.

When many say, "Just face it, your skills and experience level were just not up to par;" yet you see them bring in a less experienced person and provide all kinds of support to ensure their success; you know, oh so well, it was not your imagination. This book is not a 'color, race, or age' discrimination conversation. This story is the conversation regarding how it is possible to 'no longer fit' after 'fitting' enough to get and keep the job successfully for some time. But, now, you have reached the plateau where the 'fit' is more critical than your success to date and potential. We invest in those who 'fit.' So, how is it that one can be a good 'fit' with promised career growth potential, and less than a year or two after accepting the offer, your growth potential disappears?

Performance discussions designed to allow individuals to get a pulse on their contributions and adjust where necessary have lost their luster. The purpose of these discussions is to learn from your leader what you do not know. It should be a powerful coaching/mentoring moment. Aware of your desired development and the organization's strategic and tactical direction, your leader should be able to guide you for your benefit and the benefit of the organization. These conversations should always be a win-win scenario. Yet I started asking what could I do to get increases and growth opportunities, and the response was, "Keep doing what you are doing." My mind's response was, *I am glad you want me to keep doing what I am doing. However, I don't want to keep getting what I am getting in the way of respect and salary.'* I am an achiever, and I need the next challenge to grow, be rewarded, and be held in high regard, just like my peers. No one can discourage me enough to walk away from my inheritance. What is rightfully mine, after years of giving my all to this organization, is mine. I am a team player. I also perform as a business owner, and I respect and care enough to use my resources to help those with whom I work and oversee. Yet securing 'the fit' somehow supersedes the documented performance.

I was surprised when I read all the performance reviews, I received during the last several years. I was encouraged by the comments. However, my day-to-day interactions with the author of each report did not add up. I started to understand the difference between being championed by a leader, written evidence of your performance, and the impact it has in a corporate setting. This difference even seeps into the one on one discussions with your leaders. It also impacts the assignments you receive; the training availed to you, and the opportunity to participate in external events on behalf of the company. Those sponsored are the recipient of the latest and greatest information shared at strategic tables. However, this information is not afforded to you when you are in the area of your strength and simply expected to keep that hub running well. For many, that is more than enough. They will ride that assignment out until they decide to leave, or they no longer have a choice. This scenario is not enough for an achiever. It is like a death sentence to an achiever. Am I expected to sit here and keep doing what I am doing without any opportunity to stretch my learning and experience? You have got to be kidding. We must understand our purpose overall. Why are we in these organizations? We reached the ceiling.

A great influential gentleman in my life several years ago told me that I am where I am to help people. After hearing this, I started paying attention to daily interactions and opportunities to mentor and coach individuals. In some cases, they were put in positions without any support, left to succeed or fail on their own. Some did not receive the support required because their leaders were not true leaders; instead, they were too busy climbing the corporate ladder, focused only on what was right for them. Others did not know how or did not care to lead individuals who were not like them. Their biases and the filters they operated through prevented them from building a diverse culture that supports a different community. Leadership training is for those who reach a specific position in the organization. Many hopeful individuals fight to overcome hurdles to succeed. Yet they are denied training and advancement.

More recently, organizations have developed programs for potential leadership candidates equipping them with leadership training and exposure to senior-level executives for mentoring. Kudos to both efforts. The majority of people who fall outside of the leadership development programs also need a way to overcome the many obstacles that impact work life. Some have support to make it through the barriers, while others have no clue how to gain a perspective that will serve them well in their decision process. Without servant leaders, it is impossible to be successful. Whether he or she is your immediate leader or someone you can lean on for wise counsel, everyone needs someone with a proven track record whom they can trust to be their safe place. No one knows everything. It is great to connect with those who have gone where you want to go.

I am also there to help - as the Business Ambassador. I have overcome overt and blatant sabotage and self-sabotage. It was no picnic. I learned from the good, the bad, and especially the ugly. I would not wish some of my experiences on my worst enemies. However, I am stronger because of them. I am more realistic in my expectations, and I know how to choose which battles are worth fighting. I know how to press forward, and I now have the patience to ride out situations that look and feel like they are for my demise, but they always turn out for my good. Sponsor or no sponsor, you can navigate these chilly, troubled waters successfully. How? Seek to gain clarity and a fresh perspective that helps open your eyes and heart to what is going on around you.

The real culture is what I learned, but not without enduring turmoil. At one point in my career, my leadership team was a part of a coven. I had never seen anything like it. After years of experience in the workplace, I was familiar with new leaders bringing in their team to fill in the top positions. It happens, perhaps, all too often. However, this particular group was simply weird. They were the textbook 'clan,' worshipping the leader and not attempting to display any individuality in style or thought, evidenced by their conversation and daily behaviors. Everyone drank the Kool-Aid gladly, that is, until bitten by their viperous queen. I watched as one of the coven members, one of the hardest workers, mind you, went from having high authority one day to being destroyed in reputation and respect the next day. Once recognized in the industry as a credible individual, yet because she no longer served their needs, she experienced the repercussions. From seemingly indispensable to actively dispensable, her only recourse was to leave the area and, ultimately, the company. She lost her status like a lead balloon.

This group of women had deep-rooted relationships in and outside of the office. They all entered this company from another company once the queen arrived. You know how that goes. The talent that already exists in the organization is surpassed by those new to the company. Internal movements result in similar leadership changes. One individual moved to an area within the company, and the next thing you see is a migration of their colleagues moving over as well, taking all the prime positions. They come ready to reconstruct or shift things around. The leadership team moved amongst the attendees as a tightly-knit group. They sat together, walked together, and talked together. Here was an opportunity to mingle with the teams, get to know the staff. Instead, the senior leaders represented themselves as a wolf pack missing the opportunity to interact individually with anyone outside of their circle. Very strange. This behavior demonstrated just the opposite of power and strength. It was mass insecurity. Still, in the office, bullying and constant discouragement occurred.

I would never expect this type of behavior from such critical, condescending, and degrading individuals. Where was the command of the room? Where was the confidence required of those working for you? Where was the leadership that an organization expects to see in senior-level individuals? Where was the courage in those who have worked many, many years in the workplace? It reminds me of the gang leader who walked around the high school with her squad, trying to intimidate people with her presence with an entourage—immaturity at its best from a senior leader and her team in a significant corporate environment.

The climax speech was not impressive—all of this from those who looked to cut people down at their knees. I would not wish this destructive behavior on anyone, including them. It was horrible to witness. It was even more difficult to swallow after previously working for a compassionate, communicative, reliable, knowledgeable, and approachable leader. To go from a leader who engaged the entire organization most appropriately at every level to this dysfunction was jolting. Why in the world did this happen?

The First Eighteen

The first half of my career had its share of negative encounters as well, but nothing like this. I was now dealing with the big dogs. New level, new devil!

It is true. Dorothy, we were no longer in Kansas. Looking back, up until this point, I had worked for some demanding and tough leaders; they were teachers of the business and taught me how to win and how to be the best. We received an education in business while dealing with very high-profile clients and business exposures. We always had to bring our 'A' game to win the contract and build a relationship that would allow us to secure annual contract renewals with increased product offerings. These leaders cared about the business and understood that the critical component to success is the people who are getting the job done.

Were there some crazy decisions made in promoting some over others for political reasons? Absolutely! Did some of those decisions negatively impact me? Yes. However, I felt less than or degraded so that those decisions made could be justified. I was rewarded and recognized consistently for my achievements. I felt appreciated. I was taught and learned a lot in this season. This experience was vital for me because I did not come from a business-centric family.

My parents are educators and musicians. The legacy of hearing business acumen around the breakfast, lunch, and dinner table from infancy is not my story. My journey began in college. I learned to apply concepts that were in the blood or DNA of many of my peers. I am grateful for my start in business in the first 18 years. The latter 18 years, however, have increasingly demonstrated the darker side of the company in various instances and for multiple reasons. Still, I am finding that all these years combined have taught me lessons that those newly entering the workplace are experiencing, which is very unfortunate.

At least I had the benefit of a great start in the business realm. I received excellent extensive training actively managed throughout the years by development plans. Leaders steadily looked for opportunities throughout the entire organization to help me meet the demands of my project. Leaders were actively engaged in my success, realizing that my success equaled success for the organization.

Coaching moments occurred all the time. "This went well because you did these things. Your performance can be better next time by adjusting the following." I was prepared for situations and then placed in those situations with the oversight of my leader so I could implement what I learned. They knew what they had imparted to me and were comfortable in letting me spread my wings. Without such experiences, how could one ever learn how to fly successfully? The risk they took was minimal due to the investment they made in preparing me for the task and the possible scenarios that could arise.

I am not sure what I would have done or where I would be today if I had lived these negative experiences upon entering corporate America. As a much more radical individual in my youth, I may not have ended up with the quality of life I can enjoy now. I fought hard for what was right back in the day. It did not matter who you were. I would state my case and make my point. I saw the ideal outcome from a long way off and led others to see what I saw. Often, I jumped to incorrect conclusions moving too quickly, not considering the perspective of others or gathering as much information as possible. I was a 'check it off the list as done' junkie. Over time, I matured in valuing the pursuit of knowledge that allows me to make a well-informed decision while still effectively executing and bringing projects and assignments to a close as quickly as possible.

Experience has taught me to allow others to go through the process of thinking through options derived through their investigation as opposed to leading the witness. During my maturing phase, many others received opportunities that I did not win. Was every missed promotion an injustice? I am not suggesting that at all. For instance, questions often lingered in my mind when I considered a position that required more extensive analytic skills than I had. My leaders refused my request for additional training in this area. Because I know whatever I put my hand to, I will succeed in; I wanted to grow this skill set. Still, the organization refused to invest in me. On the flip side, after being in the position for some time, the job requirements changed, and I did not have an interest in that skill. I was no longer a 'good fit' legitimately. So, I started the search for a new role.

"The mind of the prudent is ever getting knowledge, and the ear of the wise is ever seeking (inquiring for and craving) knowledge."
Proverbs 18:15 (AMPC)

What about the individual hired with all the accolades and glowing adjectives that Merriam-Webster can muster? How is it that the promised shining career dims after a few months or a couple of years? Yes, the performance was high, and, despite poor communication or no communication from their leaders, Chris was still able to succeed. And, then, to be told that he is not entirely 'fitting the bill.' Shouldn't it be taken into consideration that Chris completed the work with less information than their peers or their predecessor? How is he to reconcile in his mind that he is rated poorly by the very one who was responsible for providing current information and changes that impact the assignments? In this type of scenario, it is difficult to ignore the question, who is being the professional? Is it the one who is doing their absolute best despite obstacles or the leader failing to provide the tools necessary for success?

The position you hold does not make you a professional. You can attain the most prestigious title and lack professionalism. But the one who can get up every morning, come into the office, respect all those who think it is okay to be openly disrespectful; that person shows signs of professionalism. Professionals get the job done under the most severe adverse working conditions with quality, integrity, and accuracy that would make any CEO proud to have them on the team. Peter Barron Stark's blog post, "The New Definition of Professionalism," provides an update on professionalism in the rapidly changing world. It may surprise you that it has less to do with how you look, although looks do carry some weight in determining one's level of professionalism. I agree with Peter in his explanation of how you are considered a professional, look set aside, if

- Your attendance is consistent and timely
- You are accountable
- You are willing to go the extra mile
- You communicate respectfully with everyone
- You stay calm and focused, even in the most difficult situations
- You do not gossip and are a great communicator
- You use good judgment

Influential, effective leaders that live out these qualities day to day are professional. Members of your teams are also professional when they consistently demonstrate these qualities. If you work in conditions where professionalism is not the standard minimum requirement, when sharing your feelings of concern, you may hear individuals say, "I didn't know this was occurring." Or, "I didn't know you felt this way." Unfortunately, in some cases, you may hear, "Could it be that you may be overacting to something very innocent?" Your immediate thoughts maybe like my thoughts. "What?" Sadly, this is a realistic response within the corporate arena. Should you encounter this response, here is what I suggest:

1) Choose to educate/inform the individual who is asking or insinuating that you are making much out of nothing. Sharing

your perspective in a noncombative manner will enlighten any open mind and ear. While it may not change their behavior, it will awaken their consciousness as they experience your example.

2) Offer to partner with the individual and point out instances when these practices occur that may often go unnoticed. What appears innocent to one can be very offensive and harmful to another who experiences bias injustices.

3) You may choose not to take on the assignment of being another's consciousness or social educator. Continue to carry yourself most professionally while looking for another position in a more favorable environment. Keep in mind that there is no perfect place. However, some areas are far more welcoming than others.

My choice response is to continue representing myself professionally, providing superior service, and create great products or outcomes. I am not responsible for anyone else's development in emotional intelligence. Everyone must continuously self-reflect to identify blind spots and gaps for success. I own my progress, and others should do the same. I do not have to explain anything to anyone. Enlightenment and revelation come when one seeks information and new perspectives to grow.

There is nothing more disheartening than a leader who is glaringly and possibly intentionally oblivious to your cry for growth. As my leader, should you not be aware of my desired development opportunities and inform me of potential possibilities? Please understand you must own your development. However, I think that the pendulum has swung too far to the left as it pertains to self-development. Lack of guidance leaves the individual to "fend" for themselves, which can lead to frustration. There must be a healthy balance of an individual's purpose and opportunities provided by leadership. The organization benefits when leaders help the individuals grow and nurture their goals for the good of the individual and the organization. It is a win-win.

The administration has information for trending, upcoming initiatives, and future restructuring that creates gaps that could be filled by individuals in the organization that match the skills needed. However, some leaders have abandoned all participation in the development of their team. It appears the attitude is one of "just get the job done where I've placed you." Even when initiating the conversation for assistance and greater awareness, the response has been, "just keep doing what you are doing." How is this helpful feedback for the individual seeking growth?

In my experience, this is code, meaning; I am not helping you advance. Limited or lack of feedback is clear evidence that you do not have sponsors advocating for you. It reminds me of my 'why' for being here and how I can use these experiences to help others and search for areas where I can further enhance while waiting for what is next.

I am still learning the deeper dynamics of business, mindsets, personalities, and situations. The scenarios differ with circumstances, characters, and my increased awareness. It is fascinating to watch myself evolve as all factors in play change. Timing and external and internal organizational challenges influence the approach and outcome of any situation. It may feel like you have been in a particular scenario before. However, due to the slightest variance in the elements of the equation, you cannot draw a conclusion quickly based on assumptions.

Consider all aspects of the situation, even if it ends up as you expected; how you got there may be quite different from before and for various reasons. Nothing is a waste.

Until you are clear on what is next and the provisions you have for you to move forward, learn, and grow where you are. Help those who are in your sphere of influence so they can avoid obstacles.

A Fresh Start

Rob, a young junior manager, new to the organization, finds himself cut off from promised advancement. He is unaware of outside opportunities.

Where is the promotion guaranteed? Where are the support and coaching described during the interview process? The next level escapes him. This inequity does not make sense to him.

Rob completed his assignments on time, even when he carried the most massive workload on his team. He covered for his leaders when they were out on vacation or had more pressing assignments.

It is a fact that some of us must work harder than some of our peers for the privilege of remaining employed.

But it gets better. Rob is finally, given the opportunity to lead a team. However, he receives no guidance or leadership training. He did not know this was a pilot. Rob thought it was a new assignment.

The pilot is now, over, and he must return to his previous position. His manager's response, "Rob, you are being demoted because this is not a 'good fit.' Yet, not once were expectations shared with him, nor was any training provided. Hands down, this is a crushing blow.

As a result, Rob must fight to find the motivation to keep his head in the game until he can figure out his next steps. Leadership's gross and inadequate handling of this situation should have significant consequences; however, scenarios like these too often go without recourse, and leaders learn that this is acceptable behavior.

How could this possibly be fair, approved handling of any member of your team, not to mention the potential impact on the clients they serve?

Not Going Out Like That

The hurt and victimized posture the leadership in that area now exudes, after getting what they wanted all the long, is poor acting, visibly foolish, and insane.

Those leaders pushed, poked, prodded, and virtually kicked Rob out by making him so uncomfortable that for his sanity, he had to get out.

It is not always about who wins, but it does matter what is best for you and your family. Staying there with the craziness would not be healthy, so Rob decided to pursue openings.

Working closely with human resources, he found a place within the organization to begin again. A fresh start is a win. This time it was a lateral move.

The HR Rep 'strongly' recommended that he take the position for the new beginning. The weight lifted.

The darkness was shifted and dispelled, and pursuit of purpose was free to be explored once again as Rob shook the dust from his feet and looked to the future with new leadership, new skills, new co-workers, and unique character-building.

Gone are the leaders whom one day used him to clean up the backlog, maintain production goals without any reward, and insisted that his normal behavior was a problem.

In contrast, others continued having poor work ethics, poor attendance, and constant drama in the workplace. But Rob was the problem?

A fresh start is just what HR and God prescribed, and Rob took a new position, never once looking back.

The advice given to Rob by his Human Resource Representative was to take a job in a different department and start fresh. That's it. Though it was good for Rob, the existing detrimental leadership remained in place.

Someone else would be subject to the same malfunctioning leader. Others would have to endure the insanity that plagued that area of the organization. Many think that the Human Resource Representatives are in place to represent individual employees solely.

Excellent HR Representatives represent both the employee and the organization at all times. At times, this involves protecting the organization from mishandling any scenario. However, some organizations misuse their HR to focus primarily on leadership.

Those who could cause significant damage to the organization. These organizations influence HR Reps to make final decisions in favor of the company. Nevertheless, now is the time for self-preservation.

Take a new position! What a difference a change in leadership and work assignment can make. Rob was well on his way to a positive workplace experience. God bless those left behind.

Calling Servant Leaders

Who is prepared to successfully lead people while fulfilling an organization's vision, mission, goals, and objectives? Balance; is that important anymore? Has catering to the upper echelon and ignoring the rest of those contributing to your success, bonus check, and next promotion become the modus operandi? Leaving hopeful, young, educated, gifted, and talented individuals, in too many cases, questioning their worth. They must quickly learn the importance of being sure of their strengths while repairing their self-esteem when encountering negligent leaders. For some, it requires overcoming the regret of wasting time joining a company that never had your best interest at heart. Searching for the right opportunity that upholds the promises made at the time of hire becomes more difficult after such a bad experience.

Past experiences with poor leadership leave the individual in quite a corporate predicament. Do I try to trust the next employer, or do I go in wiser expecting similar behavior but better at playing the game? What choices do I have? The truth is that there are no perfect people or organizations. However, the more I hear about the experiences of those entering the workplace and those closer to retirement, it sounds like there is plenty of room to raise the bar of ethics, integrity, and human kindness. I sense that we have lost something at the very core of business in our society. We once served the needs of our clients/customers and staff/teams to the best of our ability without sacrificing one for the other. Servant leaders seek to understand the development goals of each member of their team. They match those goals with the organization's goals to create a mutually beneficial opportunity. Servant leaders remove obstacles and roadblocks, so their team can meet their objectives in the expected timeframe. They keep their ears and eyes open to gather the information that will help the work excel and meet or exceed expectations. Servant Leaders are members of the team also who understand that together they win or fail.

The truth is that our staff and teams are also our clients and customers in many cases. We need the heart back in business, the workplace, and the marketplace. Selfish motives will be the demise of many leaders and organizations if they do not bring the heart back into the business. Will there be difficult decisions to make still? Absolutely. The day we lose consciousness of the impact the choices we make for the wellbeing of the organization and all those impacted is the day we lose heart for what we do and why we do what we do. Most do not question the decisions. What they will question is the approach taken to implement those decisions.

For example, an organization may struggle with incorporating diversity throughout all levels of the organization. At the time of a reorganization or downsizing, are the proper levels of diversified staff protected? What is the selection process? Many of those laid off assisted/trained those left behind. If so, who will now provide the guidance? Extensive tribal knowledge is expensive to replace, and the cost is both money and time. Yes, we have technology that can accelerate learning. However, some things are by trial and error. Without a thoroughly planned and executed transition plan, people figure it out on their own. If there is no strategic plan for change, productivity will slow down.

The struggle is real, and the enemies too often go undetected and camouflaged as something or someone else. We often hear in our churches that there is an enemy to our soul. The enemy goes out to destroy your entire life. You must know that individuals and systems are used as demonic agents, knowingly and unknowingly, sometimes depending on the day or the moment of the day. The corporate growl is real. You can see the saliva dripping from the teeth of the hound dog strategically placed against you, and it stinks from flesh and blood of positions left vacant by their last victim. It is a psychological, emotional, and physical fight. Some of us have had to fight in this corporate arena.

We have wrestled day and night to survive an unwelcoming environment. Consider this scenario: my new employee, Sharon's resume and confirmed experience, were superior at the point of entry, yet once in the hallowed hallways, the negative and intimidating forces go to work to destroy her. What in the world caused the shift away from 'Sharon's amazing,' 'so polished and beautiful,' 'Sharon's probably overqualified,' 'we must offer more than what she's asking so we can get her on our team'? Everyone wanted Sharon in the company. Senior leaders actively participated in the hiring process. They tell me that Sharon will report to me. After a short period, ironically, Sharon is fighting for her livelihood, for her very existence, because of the lies, lack of support, manipulation, and unrealistic expectations drawn by those associated with her assignment. The mental abuse is unreal, data was changed without her knowledge—decisions were made without her inclusion. Information is miscommunicated to multiple channels to create confusion. The darkness thickens, and the stench of sulphur becomes strong. The snakes of confusion, disbelief, doubt, hopelessness, questions, and more questions become entangled in Sharon's head as she contemplates, "God, what have I done? I came across the country for this 'better opportunity' to get closer to home, and I have stepped into the fiery brimstone of hell. God, what have I done? My family is still dependent on me and my salary. God, where do I go? How do I survive in the meantime?"

"The name of the Lord is a strong tower; the [consistently] righteous man [upright and in right standing with God] runs into it and is safe, high [above evil] and strong." Proverbs 18:10 (AMPC)

What is Sharon's saving grace? How does this individual get through this scenario? Thank God for a praying manager. Thank you, God, for a manager who knows the power of anointing in the workplace and who takes authority in the spirit realm. The prayer warriors know how to shut down the plots and plans of the enemy. These are leaders who understand that their role is not just to lead, but also to serve and cover their team members and peers – that is a faithful servant leader.

Respect Matters

It was a horrible, sadistic NIGHTMARE! A winter morning found me at an inner-city location training center. My responsibility is to train underwriting executives and account managers in communication skills as they prepare to launch a new auto product.

As usual, the attendees sat in groups of their friends, those with whom they were most comfortable. I immediately noticed that all the underwriters (in this case, all men) sat together at one large table while everyone else sat at the other tables.

The scent of arrogance and entitlement was poignant from the side of the room where the underwriters sat. The remainder of the room succumbed to the intoxicating superiority exuded by the underwriters.

I am often dumbfounded by individuals who treat those they are dependent on as if they are inferior. If those whom you consider subordinate did not come to work every day and perform their responsibilities, you would be incapacitated. You could not be the hero you think you are in your head.

True leaders know, without a shadow of a doubt, that the team is what makes the difference in real success. The capacity gained and the fresh perspective from other's input are invaluable when you are trying to maintain a competitive difference.

A consultant offers a very fundamental simplistic truth: treat everyone in the organization with respect, especially the administrative and janitorial staff. One would think that this is a given.

However, my experience proved that this lesson, once taught to children as they would greet others, has escaped many leaders and want-to-be leaders. Too frequently, I have had individuals consistently ignore me in the hallway, yet we spend hours together in meetings face to face.

Let us never be too distracted or too important to acknowledge the presence or existence of another, denying them the courtesy of a simple greeting. Hello! Good afternoon! Have a great evening! See you tomorrow! This type of simple consideration makes a world of difference in the workplace.

True collaboration involves trust, respect, and sharing. The more you trust others, the more you are willing to share. Putting your biases in check and remaining open to the strengths of those sitting across from you allows the absolute best products and services to evolve. A great place to begin is with those biases you are aware of, those we almost flaunt as medals of honor.

Biases are limiting and not intended for celebration. A bias is a preconceived or unreasoned perspective toward a particular situation, person, or group. It results in favoritism for those you are biased toward or a negative impact for those you are biased toward.

The wonderful thing that happens when you are open to new experiences is that you may become aware of any biases you have. Staying with the revealing experience openly presents you with a greater chance of getting beyond the bias to a greater you, someone far more enriched.

Working towards a greater good or common vision does not mean that you agree with every aspect of everyone involved. It simply means you desire the strengths of your partners and the wealth of their experiences to shine through so that you all benefit.

As a leader or team member, how open are you to first admit that you have biases, some of which may be almost too shameful to verbalize? Acknowledging and overcoming a bias you might have, whether it is towards a person's gender, skin color, age, or beliefs (to name a few), is a crucial first step toward success.

A conscious bias state of mind is far deeper and, yet, much easier than undermining and underestimating the value and potential contributions of someone who meets your bias.

Operating from the premise that a woman is less significant and dispensable is an obvious and often discussed bias. What about intolerance for someone slightly older than you or with health challenges that may cause them to move slower than you?

How often are you rushing by them on an escalator, upstairs, or into an elevator without the consideration of potentially throwing them off balance?

Do you consider dads who choose to be present as much as possible for their children to be less than you or "not real men"? You may think this is noble. Not everyone values such choices when it does not benefit them.

Often, it is the young guy who is single or married without children who receives preferential treatment in assignments, salary, and shared information. Why?

They believe they have "less baggage." One can only assume the thought is, 'It is easier to have those who are more like me closer to me because I can predict their behavior based on the bias I hold.' The truth is that having and holding onto bias will limit and destroy potential growth in both the one who has a bias and the one who receives it.

What about the hidden bias within departments and positions? For example, if my job requires more critical thinking and judgment, then I may consider those who gather the information, rate my product or service, and package my proposals to be of less importance.

Those gathering the data, rating, and packaging use extensive critical thinking as well. There is no room for first-class versus second-class citizens on a team. No big "I" and little "You." How does it benefit the process for any one person or group to look down on others, especially when you depend on them for 80% or more of the process toward winning the deal?

On the other side of the coin, why do we let the opinions of others formulate our definition of ourselves? I suggest that we are not clear and confident in our identity and the value we bring to the organization without validation in a performance appraisal or conversation.

The fact remains that you can find yourself in a position where your strengths and contributions are never fairly publicly acknowledged.

Leaders and peers ignore the contributions you make. Or where a different picture is painted to keep you where they need you while preventing your growth.

Such injustice may be in the form of written performance evaluations or behind closed doors as they make decisions regarding salary, bonuses, and new opportunities. Which scenario can be worse? They are both detrimental to a career.

Yet the unwritten, behind closed doors conversation can leave you wondering, 'My appraisals say one thing, but the rewards and benefits are non-existing. My one-on-one conversations sound promising and thought-provoking, yet upcoming new opportunities are shared with my peers and kept from me, even when I ask.'

It is interesting when leadership feels it is warranted to leave me out of critical conversations that change the direction of my assignments. The crazy thing is that this happens even when my assignments are their direct requests.

Certainly, they needed what they initially asked me for; otherwise, why did I get the assignment? Wouldn't they want it completed quickly and correctly?

However, I received the requested information much later than necessary and incorrectly because they failed to see the benefit of maintaining close, relevant communication with me regarding the assignment.

Respect matters, regardless of personal or professional differences. Let's respect one another at a minimum for what we all bring to the table. In our positions, we have gained expertise that we all will benefit from when the deal goes through in our favor.

After all, I am sharing experiences with my peers about the work we do, just as you do. The culmination of experiences yields more informed decisions and is an immediate result of analysis and conclusions drawn in collective lessons learned.

Being intentional about the look on your face as I speak in a meeting may just make a difference in the opportunity for you to build a stronger, more profitable relationship with OUR client. Do not assume that anything your peer has to say is stupid, requiring clarifying commentary from you every time they speak.

This perspective was my encounter. But they had not walked in my shoes, so they had no idea the insight that I brought forth, yet they so readily dismissed it by talking over me or not even inviting me into the room to discuss the strategy.

I am or should be an equal partner here and demand that I am respected. My voice counts. It always has, and it always will.

As you go about your projects, assignments, or presentations or sit in on someone else's, remember the rule of respect.

In the corporate setting, we must do better at giving respect if we should desire to attain it for ourselves.

Misfit or Agent of Change

Either way, I looked at it; both, being a misfit or an agent of change, are extremely uncomfortable and causes me to long for the opportunity to take a deep breath to get relief. Can a Sista get a break?

Even on purpose, there were many times when I desired to be among those who understand and get me, yet I was in situation after situation, challenging the status quo and making folks uncomfortable; in some cases, not even knowing why. I felt like a misfit.

I was once called a misfit by a leader. Many times, it was a result of asking questions or having expectations that people, primarily leaders, were not ready to deal with the conversation. Digging up old bones and habits that they did not have to confront. They lingered in styles and behaviors, often rearing their ugly heads, yet nothing caused them to face themselves and, at the very least, acknowledge that this ugliness existed.

Challenging the status quo is difficult for everyone involved. I was a change agent in these cases, reflecting on individuals the behaviors that were not healthy for the team and overall objectives.

Ironically, I know what it feels like to have a negative trait revealed through self-reflection of observation by others. It has happened to me plenty of times, causing course correction. I could not stand the stench of not facing my "ugly." It was too potent to ignore.

God is also inside of me. He is calling attention to what he is ready to purge, heal, and replace with his goodness. Many learn to ignore his voice. Ignoring him is too painful for me and far more work than I desire. Though not the most popular choice, the wisest thing to do is to face the truth, stop the devil, and be free.

I spent far too many years in bondage. Once I learned the sweet fragrance of deliverance, it was a beautiful thing. No, it is not ever easy, but when you are "sick of yourself," as I have been plenty of times, you are ready to move on no matter how uncomfortable those around you may be.

I have learned that many will see you running full force to your death, yet they like you better in your mess because they understand you in that state.

Peers, co-laborers, and, at times, leaders do not know what to do with the new you. The reinvented may also cause you to be considered a misfit. You choose to think differently to become more productive, to become healthier, and to enhance your life. What appeared to work before is no longer working for you, and the disfunction it caused is all around you.

That is when you no longer fit into their reality of you, into their group, into their truth. You cannot change because they do not want to change. They were happy just as they were, or maybe they did not know how to break free.

The truth is that many do not know that breaking free is even an option. You do not have to remain combative, confrontational, overly sensitive, rude, manipulative, dishonest, overly critical, judgmental, disrespectful, or self-righteous.

Honestly, my break for freedom was not a strategic well-thought-out plan from my perspective. It was nothing that I controlled or planned. I just knew it was more dangerous for me to remain self-righteous and judgmental than it was to leave the bondage.

There were governmental rules that I was violating by staying in my condition. God said enough is enough. It became evident that my time was up when a young man whom I ministered to as a youth in the church saw me in the hallway after exiting the sanctuary and said, "Mrs. Owens is still here?" To me, Tony was expressing his surprise to see me still doing the same thing I was doing before he went away to college. It was as if Tony had a greater expectation for me than I did for myself.

When he left for school, I was recommending much change in that church, good changes, especially for the youth. My success did not come without resistance from the well-entrenched regime. Tony experienced my success time after time, introducing new programs and ideas. Yet to his surprise, I was still running the same programs I had started four years prior.

He was disappointed based on the tone of his question. I felt that question deep in my core. I never answered, but I understood later that spiritual shifting was taking place in my life. The change was coming to bring the Change Agent back to life in me.

The truth is that all hell broke loose at that point. The reality is that all hell broke loose in my life years before that as I was under the control of demonic influences that lead me to lifestyle choices that I never thought I would make.

I have learned never to say never. I have learned not to be judgmental. Most importantly, I have learned that I cannot live this life on my own without the grace of God. I need every provision he has already prepared for me through his son Jesus to thrive in my purpose.

The harshness and intimidation that resulted from my behavior impacted the way I lead my team. Under the premise of protecting my team and me, I demanded excellence.

The truth is a good character trait turned sour. Change at an exorbitant rate and drive added unwarranted stress on the team. Desiring excellence is not bad. Obtaining excellence at the cost of the sanity of those around us is bad. People need space to grow and create excellence.

No one is perfect, especially the self-righteous ones. I could not and no longer wanted to "still be here" producing as a bull in a china closet in the spirit of getting it done.

I do not have to have all the answers. There are a wonderful grace and freedom that comes as we allow the pure tapestry of our thoughts and performance to create what none of us could ever create alone.

Fight to Remain in the Game

This period in my life was another hard time, an extremely uncomfortable place. It felt as if nothing was going right for our team. We received complex assignments yet only received partial information. Critical information was not shared with us until something blew up in our faces, or it was shared extremely late, causing us to work extremely hard to recover and make necessary adjustments before production.

The team headed for its demise. I do not think any of us had a clue what was happening. I know I certainly did not. There were only a few of us remaining from what some had termed "the dream team."

Yet after shifts in leadership, the team was dispersed for the most part. Still, I was surviving as the lone soldier on a team that previously competed against us, most professionally, of course. But the subtlety in repositioning and blatant disbanding reshaped the program with the younger folks at the helm and the more seasoned crew providing expert insight.

If upper management's strategy is to do things differently and become more innovative, the apparent assumption is that the older workforce, those who have been in the trenches blazing trails, is now a liability. Is it true that they are so entrenched they may not have the foresight to move in a new and exciting direction?

This perspective is presumptuous and debilitating to a team. Why can't creativity and longevity come together to make explosive changes? A successful corporate environment will value each attribute for its contributions and not simply discount one over the other. For too long traditional business has modeled and promoted the genre of teamwork, yet its rates, ranks, and rewards are based on individual contributions. Isn't that an oxymoron? Here is a novel idea: if the effort required a team to work consistently in unity with high quality, then performance should be based on the same.

It is funny; many years ago, the peanut butter approach to rewarding teams was prevalent. For those who might not be familiar, the "peanut butter spread" was a system in which rewards were spread thinly but evenly among team members.

Everyone, or the majority, received some slice of the pie. Years later, the notion shifted to give significant rewards to those whom the organization deemed worthy of investing in, which meant fewer members of the team would receive increases. The problem with this shift is that now we work in complete team environments, no one greater than another, because we all have different roles.

The organization deems those invited to strategic tables greater than them all. Who set up this crazy corporate world? Amazingly enough, it is our integrity that causes us to take ownership and play our role well. We never know if we will receive recognition beyond collecting a salary.

What environment would not take advantage of team players that have a high sense of integrity, pride in the quality of work, and compassion for those who may be struggling and requiring help?

As a team player, if I have the information one is looking for, why wouldn't I help? So many do not see it the same way, however. Could it be that the focus is the reward model instead of the project outcome?

Regardless of the reason, they are hedging their bets and playing it safe by holding information close to their chest. This approach is the epitome of the 'me, and just me is all I am looking after' mentality. How sad! Contrary to popular belief, this mentality will stunt your growth more than it will help you elevate.

What's more, this reward model and self-gratified mentality will have a person questioning. For example, I must attend a meeting twice a week, where I engage in an identity exercise each time. I ask myself, am I sure I know who I am and my value?

Trying to build self-confidence in a room full of peers whose language is one of superiority is very hard. Why is that? Why do they feel the comments of others in the room are so much more valuable than mine? I am positioned at the table properly. (Check). I speak in a collaborative tone. (Check). I am fully engaged in the meeting. (Check). I am the one working closely with the customer. (Check, check).

Afterward, the facilitator or leader asks my peer to validate my comments, questions, or thoughts. My peer indicates that I said it well. I do not need that internal validation, but some feel they do need to validate me because they have a clear bias that penetrates their language and interaction with me. Can I control that? Do I even want to? Nope, it would be counterproductive. It is his loss and, ultimately, the company's loss as well.

Boy, was that meeting quite a workout! It was a mental exercise involving the psychological fiber of my being. The fact that I can NOW come away from experiences like this unscathed is only due to the grace of God that caused me to mature and not commit career suicide because of these encounters.

Perhaps it is also Holy Spirit's promise that He would be with me everywhere and in everything. (Ephesians 1:23) I specifically asked Him to go with me to the board room, and He was an excellent escort. 'Keep pushing, keep stating my case, remain calm even when others are explicit in 'attempting' to shut down my suggestions.'

It is necessary to understand that you cannot confront these situations with your strength. There is a need for self-reflection and mental preparation before encountering those with a bias against you. Are they going to be open enough to consider suggestions so you can work together toward a solution, or will they be more focused on who is speaking? Are their biases preventing them from engaging fully in the conversation?

These mental workouts have often wasted away half a workday, but I come out prevailing. I know who I am. I know what I bring to the table.

I also know what I am not and what I am not trying to be. Regardless of how they viewed me consciously or subconsciously, my name is victory, and they will see how victorious I am. But, even if they never realize it, I am grateful for where the experiences have led me.

I now see them as work out equipment used toward strengthening and reinforcing who I am and whose I am — great people building great people.

Why Clarify What's Already Clear?

It was performance review time, and self-evaluations were due the week prior. We were presented with a pre-meeting question, "Did any of you complete your self-evaluation yet?" I responded, "Yes, I did." The guy next to me (also the designated leader of the team) indicated that he had not.

Naturally, the individual asking then classified me as an overachiever. The 'designated leader' asks, "Are you are looking to see if anyone else has not done it?" The individual asking says, "Yes." Am I to once again accept yet another label spewed out simply to help others feel better about their inadequacies? I will not allow unwarranted names. I am an Achiever; studies have confirmed it.

Not knowing how others feel about you may cause those corporate enemies to plague your mind if you are overly dependent on the approval of others. Should you need to know how others feel about you? Perhaps.

However, it is more important to build your self-confidence and self-esteem. Take time to access and acknowledge who has real power over you. Maybe I gave too much power to others because of their positions. Rank and position have their place, but they should not consume and define you. Know yourself and be true to yourself.

Is it me, is it them, or is it those enemies trying to create frustration, rage, or an outburst so that I abort my assignment? Inside of me, I just want to scream, as I am sure you might too. So many times, I've wanted to react in this way: "Don't talk to me that way. How can you respond to my question by leading with, 'Well, that doesn't make sense...'?' The team is experiencing something, and the immediate response is, "Well, that doesn't make sense..."?

Would that be the same response if someone else asked? Respect my time of service to this organization and the work I have done. I have worked hard. No, I do not look like you or talk like you, but my experience and thoughts count. I have been in the trenches, discounted by leaders and peers until I jumped higher hurdles and crossed more profound valleys than those who sat beside me. I am kissing retirement on the nose, and I just want to scream ... NO MORE!

No more passive aggression, knowingly or unknowingly, or comments like, "You did that?" What exactly is meant by that? You never expected me to be able to depict scenarios or decipher an email in a visual representation that others who are unfamiliar with the subject could understand. Really? Why not? HELP ME, JESUS! BREATHE.

Why does Philip have to follow up on everyone else's comments with more "clarifying comments"? Did the group need to hear that additional information, or were they already clear? No one asked for justification. Why am I upset that he feels the need to clarify or add to the thought process?

When someone feels they need to explain what was already clearly stated, it sounds as though I did not get there on my own, as if I was dependent on that other person. (This was not the case.) It also undermines the person speaking and takes away from their credibility. Dear God, I hope I have not done that to others in the past. If I have, I apologize to each one of you.

How demeaning to have Philip come over the top of my comments adding commentary that is not necessary. It only strokes his ego, that competitive ego, saying, "Yes, I was a part of that, too." Really? Do not let these situations or people steal your confidence, which is what can happen if you allow these actions to take root in your soul and psyche.

It demonstrates that this individual does not have any confidence in your abilities. You have lost credibility with that individual. The individual wants to be the voice of authority. Is it worth the fight? It depends on where you are in your career, your goals and plans within the space you are in, or your proven track record.

Moreover, everyone seems to know what is happening in your area other than you. Were you excluded from conversations, but you still are expected to respond? Voices tell you not to say anything unless you know what you are talking about, yet there are millions of people who have made careers out of speaking incorrectly on behalf of the work or teams.

When someone shows themselves to you, believe it. Stop hoping that things will change without real change initiated by that individual.

My entire career, I fought for my place and, for the most part, it has been leadership I've had to deal with for fair treatment. I am not talking about the leaders who, In those rare cases, truly nurtured and helped me to grow, showed me the ropes, and coached me for growth and advancement.

But in the matrix environment where individuals are responsible for the work you do but are not direct management, it gets weirder. There is no need to compete with Philip. He is already the chosen one. Philip was put in a position to lead, although he does not know how to build or support a team.

The next day, after that awkward mess of "clarifying comments," I felt much better. What a difference 24 hours make. Of course, I have not encountered the enemy forces of competition or grandiose spirit — enough of how others knowingly or unknowingly can make you feel. The key to survival is to ensure that you keep your emotions in check. Know the root cause of the issue and choose your response wisely. The attack is real.

I'd Rather Go at It Alone

The atmosphere and fine dining were quite pleasing, yet the venom that spewed throughout our conversations made the room dark and gloomy. The food became distasteful. I could not point to any single area that was worthy of positive commentary during my mentor Carol's conversation over dinner. Even those whom I thought Carol held in high esteem were subject to harsh criticism. The organization's frailties were alarming for me to see through her eyes.

Naivety was not the issue. I wrestled the entire evening with the fact that I still had several years before retirement, and I was unsure how to survive, let alone succeed, in this degrading environment. Carol was among those privileged, she was a well-respected, and sometimes feared Vice President. She was suffering on the inside, so how was I to rise above the mayhem as an inside outsider?

The information I needed to excel or, at a minimum, move forward was not available from the very one who agreed to show me the way. I left dinner feeling like a dump yard and vowed never to subject myself to that type of interaction ever again. It was not worth any imagined benefit.

Mentor or executor, I could not tell the difference. What I did know was that it was not healthy nor required for me. I was determined to find a better way. This breakthrough took several years of exposure to manifest. Why? I have no idea. All I knew was that Carol continued to express the desire to help me, yet it never came to pass. When you need help and you have no other options, you go with what you know until you wake up and realize that it is not working.

I chose to go it alone. I would rather go it alone, even if I had to struggle. I did not want this poison in my psyche, nor did I want to continue to hang onto false hope. It had been proven more than once that advancement was not coming my way with the help of Carol. It was made clear after being passed over for a position given to one less desired but politically connected. Ironically, defeat was not my demeanor.

Instead, I looked for a fresh start. In doing so, a hiring manager gave me an enlightening response when I asked, "What happens when this project is over?" Peter responded, "Any time you do a good job on an assignment, other assignments will be made available to you." Freedom came at that point.

Freedom, going from depending on Carol sponsoring me to solely relying on my performance to make room for me. Was it at the cost of more visible, higher-paying positions? Was it in the protection of the sanctity of my sanity and value system? Sponsorship may be unavoidable, but what do you do when it is not accessible? Keep performing. It is difficult for people to deny the results you achieve. Keep going after and getting win after win. The production will cause people to notice.

Some people seek validation by the amount of fear and intimidation they inflict on those around them. They keep their victims close and in their circle because exerting power over them becomes a sport.

Speaking harshly, condescending, degrading, and all types of negative comments consistently break down others' self-esteem and self-image. It does not matter how strong we think we are to withstand the attack. In all reality, those attacks chip away at our psyche.

They are fiery darts piercing our very souls. Workplace abuse should never be tolerated, certainly not for any length of time. If the individual cannot be confronted in the hope of their behavior changing, then it is best to get out and move on with your life. Stop ingesting poison that will eventually kill your confidence and future potential. Again, do not think it is not affecting you. Those wounds go deep, especially when repeated daily. Often you do not realize the bondage you have been in until you are free from the chains of abuse.

I am free. No more hostility, abuse and neglect from my leader, Carol. I could not ask a question without walking away, feeling as though, somehow, I should have miraculously known the answer. The weird thing is that she is repeating what she experienced. It is behavior that trickled down from the top. It is considered a badge of honor. Inflicting the same pain onto others, no matter how dysfunctional.

Hurt people are hurting other people. Strong leadership that supports me while stretching me for the next challenging opportunity would be ideal. But the beauty that can come from this ugly is that leadership dysfunction is a sure way to build your character and maturity. It gives a much deeper meaning to "taking the high road" or "rising above." Surviving such abuse increases the elasticity of heart and strength.

If you are under dysfunctional leadership, do not ignore what you are gaining – endurance produces character, and character produces hope (Romans 5:3-4).

"The hiring manager offered you the job," Carol said as I stepped off the elevator. We walked off to the nearest window overlooking the eastern side of the city. I glanced, for a moment, out the window, looking for my response to her follow-up question, "Are you going to take the job?"

I had said I would go at it alone (without "sponsorship") that final night during dinner in the thick, weighty, dark, and hopeless atmosphere. Here was my opportunity. As I confirmed my desire to move forward to this new position, Carol's body caved in quite noticeably. I wondered so many times afterward if I was that important to Carol, why didn't she do more for me? Why didn't she make sure I received what I deserved, what I earned?

I was released from this assignment with a fresh new start, with exposure to the entire enterprise and a great team of people desiring and appreciating my leadership. What a great experience that ultimately led to wonderful friendships and support. We all grew professionally; I grew as a stronger leader and my team as stronger technicians, as well as those who found their way to positions of a better fit.

People assume you should have sponsorship. If you have sponsorship, you should be aware of it. Your relationship with your sponsor is one you want to groom and allow you to mature naturally through regular interaction. If you have sponsors and you do not know it, then it is ineffective.

The sponsors should share ways to become more successful in the culture. They make you aware of the land mines as well as valuable connection points. I once had a sponsor when I served as a youth leader in the church, where I introduced much change. A gentleman working with the team in support of the youth had a great influence on the pastor. He shared the benefits of the programming with the pastor and the evidence of our success.

I did not know he was speaking on our behalf until we received approval to continue the ministry at a time when the leaders of the church were threatening to shut it down. We worked great together, and I appreciated his advisement and support when it counted most.

Cobra in the Conference Room

This woman hid behind her title and authority. She wore them both as a shield of weaponry, ready to assault even the kindest "Good Morning!" or the most innocent of clarifying questions.

The Cobra entered the conference room only to be heard and to interrogate harshly for the fun of it. Only the inner circle could respond to her planted questions. How can one compete with those who have been spoon-fed and set up to win?

How can one advance past those who are coached and mentored over dinner, at the country club, at their kid's games or church bazaar? How can one rise with the swelling tide if left on the riverbank without a boat or paddle? Why is this happening when our priority should be to fulfill the vision and mission of the organization?

Some have, and some do not have. Some are informed, while others receive what is necessary to complete the task at hand. You get any additional helpful intelligence through underground relationships you have developed if given the opportunity.

If you are unfortunate enough to be visibly marked, you are on your own because no one wants to associate with one who is set up to fail … the one who is set up to "come down a notch or two."

You are the example, the scapegoat. In some cases, not even HR will help you. The very people you think you should be able to run to, also work for the company and its leadership first. The employees are second, if necessary. To whom do you turn? You hope and pray for an "off the record conversation" with someone who is in the 'know.' The information they provide, you find yourself grappling with just to survive another day. To whom do you turn?

The HR Representative, Jackie, and I interacted quite frequently as we worked together to prepare documents and reports to reflect the status of my staff. Workforce planning, for example, gave us the perfect occasion to consult. There were moments when I would stop by to discuss my development potential.

I learned that there were concerns with my performance during an interview with the Cobra, Jill. Jill mentioned specific deficiencies that no one else had ever mentioned before this conversation. My performance documentation did not mention problems with my performance.

My performance evaluations were quite favorable. Yes, some developmental areas could be improved. However, nothing matched what I heard in her office. It took me off guard in such a way that I questioned, "Why am I just hearing about this now?" "Why was this not addressed in my appraisals or even in my mid-term review?" Wait for it. Jill's response, "Well, I am addressing it now."

Note this was not early in my career. At this time, I led a team of more than 20 individuals. I had never experienced anything like this in my entire career. I was so devastated that I had to check with various leaders throughout the organization to determine the validity of the information I received. Was I in delusion?

It didn't make sense that this leader would choose to discredit me in an interview using information that should have been shared with me in a regular one-on-one meeting with my manager or, at the very least, in a quarterly development plan discussion. Jill chose to bring up incorrect data to rule me out as a candidate.

When consulted, my immediate leader, Jack, recounted conversations he had with Jill that were misconstrued or turned around for her agenda. Jack was clear on what he said and the context which he provided to Jackie, my HR representative, which, in turn, was passed on to Jill. Who got it twisted, Jackie, or Jill? I don't know.

Was Jackie put in a situation too difficult to avoid and survive? I don't know. I do know that it caused me to seek counsel from trusted leaders in the organization. Those whom I knew would be truthful and let me know where I missed it if that was the case.

I thank God for my colleague, Vicky, who was an officer of the company. Vicky advised me to go and ask leaders whom my team supported. "Ask them how you are doing," she said.

I immediately scheduled meetings with several leaders. I respected their candor, which reaffirmed me but also coached me on how to improve my visibility and begin to change my position.

I do appreciate comments such as, "Yvette, what are you doing now? I know what you were doing when you were in your old department. I don't know what you are doing now.

We see your team, but not you." Let me share that there was a reason for the lack of visibility. I managed my team from behind, so the leaders who respected and trusted me could learn to work with and depend on those we brought into the organization to service departments across the division.

I never contemplated that this strategy would negatively impact my growth potential. It never crossed my mind. Hidden, I managed and supported while being undermined and disadvantaged before my leaders.

This was a formula for defeat and loss at my expense. But my consistent performance and reputation proceeded me, making the plots and plans against me difficult to stick and eradicate me.

A reorganization allowed me to start over in a new position. It was not a fresh start because my new leader, Brenda, was still under the control and in the dark circle of Jill. Nevertheless, unknowingly, I was getting closer to my time of release from this leadership team.

Success Is Personal

Kelvin came in every day, and sat at his desk with his head down, managing his accounts. He was a robust technical professional, respected for effectively maintaining healthy relationships with all levels of key stakeholders — a practical and well-rounded teammate in minimizing risk and making a fair profit. No one wondered if Kelvin would show up and perform in stellar fashion. He always did. He was very humble, never blowing his own horn. He simply trusted that the right people would notice and move him into an even better position. But no one did.

No one tapped him on the shoulder with great news of a more challenging assignment. Why would they, when there were sharp, consistent, quiet technicians (like Kelvin) on the team, never requesting anything more?

I was sure that Kelvin expected them to notice and "do right by him." It never happened. I perceived the scenario from my definition of success.

I desire continued growth through advancement and salary increases. Was Kelvin content doing what yielded him a decent level of professional respect and paycheck? After all, in those days, many perks came with the position; lunches paid for by suppliers, destination planning conferences at least twice a year, holiday parties, and the like, all paid for by the firm.

I did not appreciate the need for trustworthy technicians who paid the price through training and exposure to exceptional case management. It takes several years to build that skill. Kelvin was content in conditions that were not satisfying to me.

We clearly defined success differently. It is possible to reach a plateau when you don't take on new challenges or create visibility for the work you do well so that those who make promotion and increase decisions will remember your face at the critical annual decision point.

In either case, some choose to plateau, and others stay too long and are automatically plateaued due to age, being unfit for the desired workforce profile, not connected, or simply not liked enough or at all to cut.

Fighting for my place at the table as I climbed the ladder to success created an over-sensitivity to any opposing comments made toward my points or ideas. I was fighting for my life, my mere existence, to continue to earn a living while regaining dignity in this space.

I did not see the degradation of my value in the organization coming. It appears while I was taking care of the responsibilities given to me, I lost sight of the strategic efforts to maintain a viable workforce at the expense of those maturing and perceived to be preparing for departure.

When asked about my plans, I did not have an answer because I did not know. Out with the old and in with the new.

Requesting more challenging assignments and inquiring what I could do to be positioned for more pay and a higher position only resulted in roadblocks and dead ends.

The issue with that is it was not yielding the desired results. I knew it, and so did they since I consistently asked. So, one can only assume that they did not care to disrupt the strategic plan in support of fulfilling assignments for me.

This situation is the backdrop which caused me to receive the following comment as a negative one. I had just presented an idea to a team of peers and superiors. Don said, "Sorry for putting a wrinkle in the conversation, but that's what I do. " Really? My heart sank. I do not know, but somehow, I felt this was a layup for him to self-promote at my expense.

This was proving yourself and your value at the cost of healthy collaborative conversation and teamwork. Not that the comments were not needed, but the intent to elevate oneself completely shifted the intensity of the conversation in a negative direction for no apparent reason other than self-gratification.

My defensive and survival frame of reference caused me to see what may have been meant as an innocent comment to be an attack on my effectiveness. Who owns responsibility in this scenario? Is it mine for being oversensitive or Don's fault for not being sensitive enough?

How would anyone know of the inner torment I was experiencing as a result of the realization that I was no longer considered a viable candidate for prime-time assignments?

Long gone were the days when I sat in meetings to discuss strategies to execute. Effective implementation became awkward when the desired outcomes were not shared.

Details and critical information were secret. Yet we were expected to move forward in support of a plan and organization unfamiliar to us.

Your success is personal, and maintaining a strong business network throughout the organization may prove to support your success.

Always remember that it truly is a 'small world,' and leadership within a culture is pretty well connected. They readily share information within their circle.

Networking with other leaders and members of their teams could very well give you the insight you need to be successful.

You will be amazed at the result of a conversation over coffee or tea.

The Environment Shapes Your Choices

We went through so much together. I experienced direct blatant racism via racist notes left in my locker almost daily. Yet Laura stood by me, befriending me as a best friend. While traveling with the band in Canada for a competition, we found racist notes under my hotel door. Once again, Laura was fantastic through her encouragement and comfort.

This situation was nerve-racking. I was alone with students and school leaders, yet someone in the group hated black people and took the opportunity to let me (the only black on the trip) know it. I found consolation in my friend's courage to not waiver in her commitment to me.

Laura and I hung out at each other's homes throughout high school and remained in touch throughout college, checking in on one another. Of course, Laura attended my wedding. She and the guy I married were close. Laura and her siblings were an extension of my family.

The phone rang. Laura called to tell me that she was getting married. I was so excited for her, and then she announced, "We will not be able to visit each other because my husband is a redneck and doesn't like black people." I did not freak out. I received it as if I expected it that day. I am not sure why I did not have more of a reaction. Laura was the only person who experienced firsthand the injustices and discrimination I received.

She was the person who remained my friend through the most impressionable years of a female's life. Here we are working our way into independent living, and my friend tells me I cannot visit or meet her racist husband. Laura meant that thing, too. She never introduced me to her husband, nor was I ever in his presence, yet somehow, Laura and I remained friends. I am not sure how that works in a person's head to be a reasonable response. I do not know how it is okay to even say that to a friend, no matter how honest or authentic one is being. We were no longer in high school. Many life experiences occurred since we left our hometown to pursue our education and careers. Environments changed, and they changed us in surprising ways I would have never guessed.

I transitioned from Baltimore neighborhoods, schools, and churches to south Jersey townships, schools, and churches to only go deeper into the isolation of the white community as I attended college in New Hampshire. The highlight of each month was when the participants of the Fred Program, Black Social Workers, attended classes on campus. Most of the black students were recruited basketball players. My presence in local establishments was an event as best expressed by a young boy who informed his mom as we stood in the checkout line, "Look, mom, a real black person." Yes, I was a real black person with my huge afro perfectly groomed and shaped, getting my education in a state where most of the black people were on military bases.

New experiences and opportunities in career and education are times for excitement and high expectation; however, I often was faced with the reality that the entire world was not eagerly awaiting my arrival. Slapped in the face by opposition on all levels taught me to forge ahead over, through, and around discouragement. Thank God there was always a balance and support close by to teach me how to walk through each situation without fear. I learned to move forward despite it.

Firsthand, I received on-the-spot training on how to shake it off and not stay in a place of 'unworthiness' or 'less than' because I had someone there to tell me the real deal — who had issues and who feared a threat.

I navigated around and through the obstacle course of those daggers of discouragement, unfair wages, and promotion denials; I required the shaping of mentoring and coaching, reshaping, molding, and suggested time to develop.

Others received promotions in spite of known deficiencies. I got the label of a "workhorse" and "adaptable," completing assignments successfully where needed and when needed, yet deemed too risky, for some unknown reason, even when persistently asking, to provide enough cover for advancement.

My friend, Kathy, was retiring from her Assistant Vice President position, and she asked me to consider the role, only to find out that, after several levels of interviews, the job was withdrawn. A pure business decision, perhaps. From my perspective, just another fiery dart shot at my soul. The apology from the HR representative only provided a slight soothing balm to the blow.

"Hello, I minded my business, halfheartedly, no longer expecting the opportunity to become an Assistant Vice-President before I retire." I found myself in an all too familiar position of having to encourage myself and seek purpose even in yet another disappointment. *"Rejection is protection,"* said Elder Shane Perry. So, my soul reasons that God allowed me to see that at least I would be considered to step into an Assistant Vice-President role.

I determined that, in the long run, the position is and was too small for me. There is far greater awaiting me that will confound those who denied me the opportunity to shine in that organization. Lessons from my past taught me to step over injustice and rise to the occasion. That prepared me for this scenario and others like it.

People are our most excellent asset/ resource and should be treated with respect, honor, and dignity, regardless of their diverse background.

Unfortunately, leaders falling into the opposite mindset, and poor behavior often treat animals better than their staff or teams. If you think an individual is less than you, you treat them poorly in conversation, behavioral interaction, and even the decisions involving advancement or compensation.

Yet, so many companies plaster everywhere that they are equal-opportunity employers. Does it show up on the ground? Employer, yes, including a lifelong career. Equal opportunity for advancement? Not so much.

I made it to another day. Thank God for the support I had from some peers, staff, and a few leaders. Even with the strength to rise another morning, it was difficult to tackle another day of back-handed compliments. My team believed I was not qualified to lead.

Yet, I fought for the credibility of our value to the organization. I found myself impacted by my longevity in this environment. I remember being at lunch with colleagues from other areas of the organization, discussing a project we supported outside of work.

Overcome with the weight of the circumstances and the heaviness of trying to push past it all, I blurted out in the middle of the conversation, "I want my joy back." My free prayer was not a preconceived thought. It came up out of my spirit, a cry for help.

Joy, being a far deeper expression than happiness, allows you to keep going strong despite whatever is going on around you with a sense of hope and expectation. Circumstances drive happiness. I survived because of my joy up until this point. Yet, I felt depleted of the pillars in my strong tower. I felt as if it could all crumble at any minute, imploding on me.

My career is supposed to be quite different. I achieved much despite those who provided what little shade there could be due to the environment. We all must pick our battles. I had to perform at a level far superior to make the fight easy for me or to remain under the radar. I am not suggesting that I was the only one who had such challenges. I know this was a way of survival for me. I had to take on new assignments requested by leadership and take on the less glamorous or less visible tasks, still performing at a level that caused others to take notice.

A former manager once proved to be right when he said, "*You don't ever have to worry about working yourself out of a job. When you do the job well, others will take notice.*" Now the environment has created the need for a respite to regain my strength and composure. I needed my joy back.

In hindsight, I recognize the basis of my joy needed to align with the proper foundation: my purpose for being. I would never be successful or satisfied, focused solely on what is required to fulfill another's purpose. Settling would guarantee the destruction of self and all that I am at my very core.

The ideal formation is when all parties are intimately aware of their propulsion and can unite for a common cause, which furthers the individual and joint momentum simultaneously. I am here contributing to your vision because it is serving my view as well in some capacity. This situation is known as a win-win. But I was lopsided. The shallow mindset of big pay, large office and recognition is never the intent of our creator.

There is far more intensity to my being. I am here breathing to fulfill my purpose and destiny. Identify and put into action your goal, and no one will be able to suck the life out of you. There must be a mutual benefit. I decided to become intentional regarding the work experiences (hence positions) I desired. I developed a strategic plan to gain specific knowledge via my career by a particular date. Identifying how this knowledge would help me reach my goal and how I would benefit from each experience helped me to focus and eliminate or avoid distractions. I no longer waited for a leader to tap me on the shoulder to tell me which position I was assigned to next. I began to navigate each career move to what I defined as success.

Mutual benefit is when we both know and expect what we will get from our relationship. Anything else leads to great disappointment by the one who is not defined and has not embraced the fundamental reason for one's existence in an unambiguous, concise, strategic executable manner.

My joy returned after knowing who I am, why I am, and how I want to get there. Even with this focus, I uncover new territory and new aspects of my abilities. Growth leads to refinement and expertise, shaping my uniqueness and authenticity, which results in greater joy. I am so grateful for the awakening many years ago during that lunch.

Coming out from under the oppression of corporate slavery into a meaningful partnership serving the needs of us both to better serve those we are both intended to reach. I have my joy back, and I will never let anyone or anything else take it away. I did not like being without it, and it cost too much to get it back.

Progressing to my success was the fight of my life, a fight for my life. I know why I am here and what I am doing, and it is working out for both our good.

The Filter

Kindergarten should be a safe, nurturing, confident image-building time of one's life. It turned out to be a place of ridicule and isolation by the students for me, which was allowed by the teacher. From the very beginning of my education, I have been in settings where I was either the only minority or one of just a handful. It was my norm.

Hardly ever was I in a class with other minorities. It was a real treat if there was another student in the class that was a minority. Ironically, in most, if not all, cases, when there was another minority student, we did not become close friends because of our diverse commonality. It was just a comfort to see the validation that there are others like me in the academic world.

The objective was to make me assimilate the class majority race as if it were the real and right way to be and anything else was wrong. I was not alone. It was a pretty warped sense of security, the classic 'misery loves company.' But I did not see it as such then. I viewed it as a privilege to receive a "quality" education. The truth is, it is only a privilege if all things are equal for all students.

My kindergarten classmates started calling me 'chocolate ice cream,' which was a tease that was embedded in my soul. The teacher did not correct them or stop them. I told my parents, and the next day, my father went to the school demanding that the teacher apologize.

The next thing I knew, I was transferred to a new school. Throughout my life, my father often recounted this scenario as a funny incident, even though he immediately came to my rescue. I think it was his way of teaching me that it was not a big deal in the scheme of prejudiced acts against my people, even though it was intolerable. It was his way of preparing me to shake such situations off. Even still, it unknowingly impacted my self-image and identity negatively, though I learned to mask the pain and excel despite it.

I compare this situation to the abuse our children experience at the hand of "educators" in today's classrooms without a meaningful level of engagement from home or communities.

My dad was right in teaching me how to overcome the ignorance of this educator and my peers. I cannot imagine the depth of damage to the self-esteem and the protective walls students develop simply to survive. It hurts my heart to know that so many of our children, teens, and young adults need to have positive, affirming voices combating the negativity they hear daily.

I believe it is a systematic attack of the enemy to degrade and squash the greatness in the generations following us. I, for one, will forever be a voice that helps them navigate their destiny to defy the opposition and odds. Each experience creates the filter through which we view and operate in life. It is unavoidable.

We grow up with a cumulation of filters that we bring to the workplace, which shape our thinking, speech, and behavior. Biases are, at times, unconscious, which can take a lifetime to dismantle.

That was not the last time I would experience blatant racism in the presence of my father. Starting my career in North Jersey, I needed housing for six months to complete my training before relocating to my permanent location. We called several places to secure an efficiency or boarding room for my stay in the area. A 'kind' older woman answered the phone and told us she had a room available and that she was home awaiting our arrival. She expected us to arrive within the next 10 minutes. To our surprise, when we arrived, she refused to answer the door, pulled the shades, and made the house appear as though no one was home.

My father knew what was going on immediately while I stood asking, "Why would she do that? We just spoke with her. She told us to come." My father's response was, "She saw us get out of the car and decided she didn't want to rent the room to us." That 'kind' old lady did not want a young black female living in her boarding room. Wrong color! Wrong House!

I heard over the years the stories from my mom and dad on how they had to use separate restrooms, drink from different water fountains, and use separate entrances.

The filters created through our personal and learned experiences come with us into the workplace. Many justify elevating themselves or those from their tribe above others at all costs.

"Many words rush along like rivers in flood, but deep wisdom flows up from artesian springs. It's not right to go easy on the guilty or come down hard on the innocent. The words of a fool start a fight; do him a favor and gag him. Fools are undone by their big mouths; their souls are crushed by their words. Listening to gossip is like eating cheap candy; do you really want junk like that in your belly?"
Proverbs 18:4-8 (The Message)

Once settled into the area and my work assignment, it was my trainer, Mary (another black woman), who helped me understand the business and navigate the political intricacies of the industry.

Thank God for Mary! She did not tolerate anything less than excellence in the work I produced. She knew I would not survive a career in the organization providing anything less than excellent results. Mary undergirded me until she knew I had what I needed to return to my permanently assigned location.

Honestly, the organization was a superior training employer. Competitors waited for new hires to complete the training and then offered them positions in their companies. Many took the bait, of which some came back to tell of the tragic mistake they had made.

Culture is critical, and the culture of other organizations was vastly different. I did not need to prove any experience that others had chosen to determine that it was not all it appeared to be. I never ventured to go to a direct competitor. Adventuring across the street only to come back when the hiring promises do not pan out was not for me.

I sought to relocate back to the South Jersey/Philadelphia area. However, nothing ever came of those attempts to move back home with my family. Not one of the interviews resulted in offers, and neither was a transfer offered.

It was divine providence for me to remain here in the New England region. It is the only explanation I can find. My assignment is here, so I will be here until that is changed.

I attended college in New Hampshire, a state where the population of Blacks at the time was less than 1%, and most of them were on military bases throughout New Hampshire.

I do not know why I am always in situations where I am clearly in the minority. After leaving Baltimore and finishing high school in the suburbs of South Jersey, I felt unprepared to go to a historically black college for some strange reason.

I felt as though I would not fit in, and I certainly did not fit in my college in New Hampshire. Some of the residents of that beautiful state only experienced Blacks on television.

I mentioned earlier my authentic experience of standing in line at a local Kmart with a young child standing behind me yelling out to his parent, "Look, mommy, a real black person." The mother did not know what to say, so she chose not to say anything. I turned, looked, paid for my items, and left the store.

In those days, I wore a big afro in honor of one of my role models, 'Angela Davis.' Yes, I am black, and I am proud of it. We learned of the significant contributions that blacks made to this country and the world.

We were taught and consistently reminded of our black history growing up in my family. Lessons such as not letting anyone call you anything but what your parents named you at birth, framed my persona.

There were also a few blacks on campus. During my freshman year, I had roommates, three seniors, all of who were white. Their idea of an introduction was telling me, "*Don't think you are going to hang out with us.*"

Really ... why would I want to hang out with them? Most blacks on campus were on the basketball team. I met my best friend, Sara, an upperclassman, on registration day. Sara lived in Boston and often invited me to Boston for the weekends. What a godsend.

During my time in college, I learned that people isolated to living in and around their race, at times, do not realize when they are insensitive to others who are not like them.

There is no filter, so there are times when we must bring it to their attention. Honestly, they would treat anyone different who is outside of their immediate circle ignorantly.

I encourage people to get out of their familiar surroundings and get to know people from different backgrounds. Put aside all preconceived notions and be open to what you can learn from others, and not assume that you are the authority.

Experiencing different cultures and ways of doing things is so fulfilling and rewarding. We all bring a perspective that can enrich another person's life. Let that be our mantra to enrich and empower instead of belittling and demonizing others who are not like us.

Am I Not Audible?

What is going on? Throughout my entire career, I have not had anyone tell me that I was not speaking loud enough. On the contrary, I had people tell me that when I speak, everyone listens due to the nature of my voice. Now I have entered a zone where multiple members of the team are talking over me when I begin to speak at a clear break in the conversation as if I do not exist. It is as if I was not in the room. I am seated near a microphone. Could it be that their level of respect for an individual can impact one's senses? Is it possible that they do not see or hear someone they disrespect, no matter how close in proximity they may be? You do not see who you do not respect. You do not notice who you do not appreciate.

It became so apparent that other peers felt the need to interrupt, saying, "*Yvette is trying to jump in and say something.*" On one occasion, as I was talking, a peer, Scott, on the other side of the screen was mimicking my previous comments as he attempted to jump into the conversation and asked, "*Am I not audible?*" I see your checkmate, young man, and I accept it because, from your limited purview and perspective, it appears that the same behavior warrants a proportionate response. You may be correct in the purest of scenarios. However, until you have walked in my shoes, Scott, you will not fully understand the magnitude of effort it takes to receive the same respect and response you receive simply because of your orientation. A case in point, would we need to have this discussion at all if I were truly considered a peer instead of just someone on the team? I am just considered a person on the team vs. peer vs. colleague. The sarcasm and silence that immediately followed led me to believe that either this had been discussed among some of them or people just did not know how to respond, so they remained silent.

It is far better to be celebrated than tolerated. Who wants to be the person picked for the team just to fill the roster? Those are the players who never get off the bench. Persons who only receive the assignments that no one else wants. The new person on the team receives assignments that are invisible to senior leadership. However, someone viewed as a peer or colleague receives respect even if they are new. Peers and colleagues get opportunities to grow in the area(s) in which they desire. At some point, unknowingly, I was downgraded from a peer to just a benchwarmer. At the same time, the culture changed in that only those close to leadership were privy to organizational changes and activities. As if to say, all you need to know is what helps you do your specific task. You do not need any other information. In this circumstance, it is easy to resort to feeling disposable unless you decide to be undeniably successful, regardless of the assignment given, which is what I did.

You need to decide as quickly as possible whether you are going to be a victim, survivor, or victor. The victim does nothing to counter or stop degrading behavior. It is unlikely there was much self-confidence to begin within this scenario. No change occurs in the victim role. The survivor probably has some level of confidence. However, it erodes with a constant barrage of disrespect. Frustration sets in due to feelings of hopelessness. "*I need this job, so I'll keep quiet and express my frustration elsewhere.*" The survivor is simply happy to make it through another meeting. But, the victor! The victor either confronts the issue head-on, demanding respect or makes changes that demand respect. They rise above the situation and prove their good. Others can contribute far less and receive respect just for showing up. The victor is a game-changer.

Who stole your confidence, and what are you going to do to get it back? If there are opportunities to remain in position and outshine or shine just as brightly as your colleagues, great! Stay where you are and prove them wrong. Even better, when you determine that it is far better to compete against your last successful project, you will experience far more gratification. Hopefully, your leadership will agree with your assessment and reward you with something meaningful to you. However, there are times when the remedy is to move on to a new area or a new job. In either case, the confidence meter must rise as you engage a more commanding presence.

Is my work effort enough to be regarded as a respected peer? Must I be viewed as a leader to be an esteemed colleague? My peers with whom I work closely share responsibilities on the same team or in the same group. Colleagues, on the other hand, are professional associates, not necessarily in the same group, division, or organization. In either case, the goal is to be respected and viewed highly by both. Ideally, I would create a proven track record, causing peers and colleagues to respect me and my contributions highly. Likewise, this should translate into salary increases, promotions, and bonuses. There are times when one's marital status, family size, outside activities, residential area, education degrees, places of worship, and social media activities feeds into the compensation thought process, impacting the results. Salary increases and promotions should be based solely on performance and not what any decision-maker thinks about one's life choices or outside activities.

Is Authenticity Welcomed?

Why is it that some groups of people can respond excitably without repercussions, and we must calm down? Why am I considered passionate when stating a case? Note: being perceived as intense is not favorable in settings requiring even keel and monotones. I believe that the practice of learning how to express yourself like the majority came about solely to make those different from me feel comfortable. I am not suggesting that going on a rant or being loud and vulgar in expression should be tolerated. I am suggesting that a very jovial employee should not receive feedback to turn "it" down because *people don't know how to take you.* I am at my best when I am in a space that welcomes my whole being. All that comes with me is my culture, my faith, my choice in personal grooming and attire, my experiences, including education, my success, my failures, my hurts, and soul wounds. Being fully aware of my priority: to complete the job I must perform, I must also acknowledge that I come as a full package. This reality is the same for everyone. There is nothing discriminatory in each individual having a complete package. However, it is tolerated for some and used as ammunition against others, primarily those who have the deepest wounds and challenges due to society's treatment of them.

Learn more about me. Become equally interested in what I did over the weekend. Lean in to understand why my priorities are essential to me. Do not be afraid of my response as to where I see myself in the future. Let us collaborate to create a win-win for all of us in our "now" with each other's end state in mind. The results will be amazing. We can soar together. My intent is not to harm you or the organization. How would I ever gain from causing harm? I am in it to win, with or without your help. Succeeding with your help is beneficial for both of us, with a positive outcome and legacy as our reward. The fact remains that too often, the organization is so focused on what is in it for them they miss opportunities to become more innovative, creative, and efficient, extending into a broader client base.

When it becomes apparent that your authenticity is not welcome in an environment, you have to assess the value of staying or finding that place where you are celebrated and not tolerated. Being honored as opposed to tolerated makes a massive difference in your performance and demeanor. There is a lot less stress when your peers and leaders welcome your thought process and talk tracks. If they simply tolerate you, this will equate to unfulfilled assignments and inadequate compensation. There is a better position for you, the real you, with your experiences and knowledge. Find or create through entrepreneurship a space where your best self contributes to reshaping the world around you. You owe it to yourself and those waiting for your arrival.

Flying Solo
(Nepotism: Whose kin are you?)

New to the area, I attended a church recommended by my cousin. A church with a rich history in the region. One morning, I decided to become a member. As is a tradition in the black Baptist church, at least back in the '80s, the deacons took me in the side room for further questioning before voting (yes, they voted) to recommend me over to the membership at large and allow me to become a full-fledged member. "*Who are your people?*" the chairman of the deacon board asked. My people? What if I did not have people here? What if the Holy Spirit led me here? What if you do not like my people? Should I move on to the next church?

Many are the first in their family to enter the corporate environment. There are no friends on the senior executive team or ministry team. There are no acquaintances in the building. No one is there in the company or ministry to help avoid pitfalls. Flying solo can be frightening, especially when others are expecting us to fail because they are not sure if we can cut it or because we are considered inadequate due to our ethnicity or background.

The question on the table is, "*Will this person fit in?*" Going at it alone is stressful when you never expected to be in a corporate setting. Your path in life led you to this place. Now what? How do I navigate this foreign land? To whom can I turn? Is there any place safe for me to express my truth as I adjust or adapt to this journey?

Kyle Alexander: My parents and grandparents never finished school. I had to work and pay for my education. A corporate partnership with my school allowed me to enter the corporate workplace, earn a salary, and complete my degree. I am from Mars. Welcome to

Jupiter. The terrain is quite different. The language is one I have never heard or spoken. The hidden expectations are still a mystery. As a young black man, I am glad to have the opportunity that escapes many of my friends and family.

I have a paying job in a program that allows me to meet and talk with senior-level decision-makers. I hear of their experiences in the company and their careers. I graduate, and they offer me a permanent job. Hallelujah! What is my career plan? What are the real possibilities for me? No one is asking me these questions. I do not even know that I should ask them of myself. I'm the first in my family to have such a job. Is it my intent to enter and exit my career in this same position? What is it that I want to do? I am the only one who can answer these questions. There are disappointments ahead as a black man trying to advance in an organization that expects me to come in and remain in an entry-level position. If I do not seek advancement, it does not require additional investment in my development, sponsorship, or mentoring. Honestly, I am just grateful to get in and be the only one doing what I do until new technology makes my role obsolete. This job is a safe place for me until a change is necessary.

Sabrina Gonzalez: My family is in poverty. They barely speak English. I am the first with a college education. No one has ever made the money I am making, even in my entry-level position. The dependency on me is excellent. There is pressure to succeed for my personal needs and to help my family when possible. My siblings find themselves in a life of drama through poor choices in relationships and behaviors. Everyone in the family pulls on each other simply to survive. How do I create a new and better life for myself when I must help those in this destructive cycle? The pull on me is significant because of my new job. I am now the official resource and source for everyone due to my internal strength to push beyond my circumstances; my ability to achieve a college degree. I landed a paying position in a well-respected organization.

The pressure can be insurmountable. Can I have a chance to establish myself in this new world without the debts and troubles of others? There is no tolerance for that, so I must succeed to survive. Who in this workplace has the fortitude to understand my situation? Who has the compassion to equip me with the tools to ensure my success? Instead, I run into those who try to make my first language a barrier in the workplace. I receive assignments as if I am a second-class citizen, and my leader rejects the recommendations that I make for improvement.

There are apparent workflow efficiencies needed, yet no one sees the need to make those changes when they have me completing those tasks, which keep me in a job that no one else wants, with little to no opportunity for advancement. Technology changes will eventually eliminate the need for my assignment. No one is investing in the preparation of my ideal job, which will fulfill my purpose. The truth is that the organization that acknowledges and invests in my strengths will achieve greater success. Ultimately, I must venture out and identify my strengths and the ideal position for myself and set a plan to get there. No one will do that for me. I can continue to do whatever they give me to do, hoping and praying that I am never let go from the organization or I can control my destiny. While this position is the best I have ever had, my family's demands are enormous, and the future is unknown and scary. Do I remain in my 'safe' place? Tomorrow is not promised. I have seen good long-time employees let go. Perhaps I can ride my wave just as long, at the very least. I will deal with a new and better plan for my career when I have to, if I have to.

Rodney Jones: I never thought I would be able to live this long since many of my friends died before they were old enough to get a working permit. Now I am on a team that does not understand how to 'take' me. They do not know me, yet my past is following me in my mind into a setting that I never imagined possible for me.

I joined a team not accustomed to any minorities. All people come to work with their mental, experiential baggage. Some people only experience people of color through their local and national news. Unrealistic expectations creep into my daily experiences. I must complete assignments in noticeably short timeframes without any guidance.

At the same time, leadership informs me that a white female co-worker is uncomfortable with me in the area on the team. Mind you; there have been no inappropriate contact or incidents. Why is her uncomfortableness my issue to address and not hers? I adjust my daily habits to avoid more accusations, eating lunch alone, taking breaks apart from my team, coming into work, and focusing only on work, no sidebars. The workplace intensity increased with more information withheld from me, preventing me from doing my job well. I was put on the spot numerous times in meetings in front of my peers to respond to questions or present information without advance notice.

Trying times, coupled with several tragic situations in my family, called for desperate measures. I quickly chose to deal with family pressures over work pressures that, in my mind, we are never going to get better. The turmoil of the storms in the family is behind me. The corporate experience built my courage to pursue similar positions in more welcoming organizations. The struggle is genuine, but it did not break me. It made me stronger.

Matt Richards: I joined a company with the help of a family member. Despite the assistance, I decided it was better to travel the journey alone instead of relying on an individual who would keep me indebted for the rest of my life for any help they provided. Thank you for sharing with me the available opportunity. I will take it from here. I passed the interview and got the job. I am a young white man who cares for his mom and appreciates all the sacrifices she made as a single parent to make sure I had opportunities to be my best. Just as my colleagues above, I love my family. I am willing to do my part to support them as I build my life. So, I find myself going at it alone without family support in the building because there are no strings attached. I would rather figure it out instead of being made to feel like I owe my whole life to someone who ONLY told me about a job opening.

In each scenario, regardless of how much risk an individual was willing to take or avoid, they are all survivors. They understand the choices they are making and are prepared to live with the outcome.

Resourcefulness is at the core of every individual. Corporate enemies, racism, favoritism, and failure booby traps may make a strike but will never take them down because they always rise to fight another day. Fighting is not something they seek. There are many days they wonder if they will ever get a break. However, they will never give up, even if they are flying solo. They have overcome so much in life that corporate politics are just another thing to master, choosing to stay or not.

Every day we must decide to get into the game. We must choose the level on which we plan to play. Some days, I must play hard. On other days, I do not have the energy to take on another battle. Which battle to fight must resonate with my soul and spirit. Experience and time will teach you what actions are worth the effort on any given day. One thing for sure is that if you do not have the mental capacity to strengthen and encourage yourself, you will succumb to corporate enemies.

There are always times to be offended, degraded, falsely accused, taken advantage of, or robbed of ideas and work. Creating a stronghold to protect yourself while remaining accessible to anything good in the environment is a critical balance to master.

In the most challenging times of my career, there were always great people who sympathized with me, seeing the poor treatment I endured. My work family is multi-cultural, multi-ethnic, multi-racial, and multi-national. Those who have indeed become family can access me, and I can access them at any time, regardless of the lapse in time between our last interaction.

While they understand my plight only to a certain extent, I have come to learn that they each have their corporate enemies to conquer. It is like the beast. We learn to adapt and adjust quickly to the changes in organizational culture, which is constant.

New leaders, at any level, have equal cultural differences. New team members change team dynamics and introduce the potential of new emotional challenges to conquer. If you want to win, you can win. Giving up is when you have cashed in to lose.

Never let the dynamics of isolated environments stop you from reaching your ideal potential. Yes, you may need to relocate or move on to another organization. Keep seeking your greater good through your best self, and you will overcome any environment where opportunity awaits you.

The Power of Networks

There is no more significant weapon in the face of opposition than staying well connected through networking. I am referring to meaningful, quality networks that are in place for the benefit of all participants. Quality connections benefiting everyone is the point and purpose of finding your tribe in organizations set up for like-minded people to bond.

Each participant deposits something to the group so that, when they need something, they have the right to make a withdrawal. Those coming only to make withdrawals from the group will not last long without commitment. Commitment, in this perspective, looks different than what many may perceive. It does not mean that you forsake all others and everything for the network. It merely means you have a place in your heart for the group and will support it when possible (capacity, finances, opportunities, and connections allow).

When you are going it alone, networking is a must. Build your community and find your tribe. While you may start not knowing anyone alone, you cannot remain alone. No man ever succeeds alone. There is always a team supporting those who grow and cross the finish line. Identify the purpose of your networking.

For example, if you are looking to become a better leader, there are networks of professionals that create best practices for leaders. They stay on the cutting edge of how the most effective leaders make decisions, impacting their teams in such a way that they become high-performing teams. Likewise, there are networks of professional writers, architects, project managers, trainers, business analysts, developers, and more.

Whether you are an introvert or extrovert, networking is a must for survival in the game of creating and maintaining strong branding. People want to know what they can expect from you. You want people to think of you and call on you when they need assistance in a specific area. Being identified as one who can fill a specific need is great for career advancement and growth potential for business owners and ministry leaders.

Many times, you must learn to embrace your level of expertise and work it to your benefit. I did not always see my ability to take an idea from start to finish quickly and with quality as a benefit. I did not see it that way because I was ignorant of the benefit of those skills, and, instead, I allowed others to define me from their perspective. Many saw me as pushy or bossy or moving too fast. I remember, one time, a dear gentleman in the church where I served said, "*Once you say it, Yvette has it done so you better be clear on what you want.*" There was learning and nurturing of that skill and natural tendencies. Most people think out loud, while some indicate what they would like to see but never think it through thoroughly enough to get it done.

For many, clarity comes as they begin to see the start of the vision. Once a model is presented, then they can articulate what they meant or desired to see. My strong suit is execution. I continue to perfect my skills to deliver solutions through better investigation, inquiry, and integration of demonstrating development. Now I am paid well for getting projects completed ahead of schedule or on time with a high degree of quality, satisfying expectations by involving the visionary along the way.

I found my tribe in the professional change management association, the project management world, and among those who build strong, effective leaders. I surround myself with like-minded people on the cutting edge of my niche so I can better affect my work.

You may recall from earlier when I slightly mentioned the following situation. It was the time I applied for a position and found out, in the interview, that the person had a negative view of me based on a comment taken out of context. They referenced how I go and get things done without having the soft skills necessary to accompany the change. Not in my performance reviews nor any conversation with any leader up until this point in my career included this feedback. I came out of the interview angry and in shock. I set up a time with my leader and my HR representative and asked why their leader had this information about me, but no one ever said anything to me. They both confirmed that comments made during rating and ranking discussions were out of context.

I went on a quest to confirm or refute the feedback from past leaders and colleagues in my network. I built a respectable relationship with each of them that allowed me to go back and have this delicate conversation with them on how they viewed me even today. It had been several years since I had worked with some of them. Each shared their perspective, including recommendations on how to move forward from this experience.

I appreciated their willingness to chat and their honesty. A colleague advised that I go to other leaders with whom I worked to get their vote on my performance. A past leader informed me that he respected me for getting things done, and he suggested that I become more visible to the senior leadership. My current position kept me hidden behind my team, intentionally, so the leaders we serviced would rely less on me and more on the Project Managers.

Another leader knew the reputation of my then leadership group and immediately began to help me strategize how I could move to another more desirable area. My point is — without a strong network, that bad interview experience could have destroyed my self-confidence and ruined my reputation. Start by having coffee or lunch with someone who is doing what you want to do. Set up a meet-and-greet conversation with someone you want to get to know better. Reach out to someone in an area you would like to explore. Join associations, blog, and participate in chats that interest you. Go to the meetups and meet new people who share like interests. You have nothing to lose. If it is not what you expected or wanted, simply stop interacting with that individual or group. However, if it is time well spent, then you gained a wealth of knowledge and probably a trusted friend.

It can feel daunting to go into a new environment and begin to open up with strangers. When we allow ourselves to become vulnerable, it is amazing what we learn and create. The information you receive in a setting is not earth-shattering or new, but you are always enriched by your interaction with others, even when it is not a positive experience.

I recently facilitated a workshop at a conference for entrepreneurs. During lunch, those at the table where I was sitting began to introduce themselves to one another. The consultant who also spoke at the event found it necessary to define what I do after I introduced myself. I immediately felt uneasy, as if attacked somehow.

After a time of reflection, I realized she was differentiating her services from my services by boxing in what I could provide the potential clients at my table. I walked away, vowing never to let anyone define me or my business without a rebuttal and correction.

What she did not know was that no one at the table was an ideal client for my business, so her attempt to knock me out of the competition was unwarranted and wasted. Not the most positive experience, but I am better for the experience, and, I received a gift that day.

Rules for You vs. Rules for Me

Some organizations provide summer employment and internships. Employees are encouraged to share openings with their children. One summer, I found an available position that would be an excellent match for my daughter.

The opportunity was in the same department I worked in; however, my daughter would report to a leader for a different team. A recruiter for the program called me one afternoon to ask about my daughter getting hired in the same department I worked.

I explained that I would not have any influence over salary, over her, or other HR decisions. I was highly offended because I could recount times when I had to make up or find assignments for a Vice President's son who would work for us, and I didn't even have the opportunity to interview or meet the new hire before his first day.

They told me he would arrive on a specific date expecting work assignments for the summer. However, my daughter had to go through interviews and be selected by the hiring manager.

Human Resources accused me of nepotism. Not all things are equal. Some have their time and work ethic, including an explanation for the number of times they have used the restroom.

In contrast, others can roam freely, visiting friends across the enterprise without completing their assignments. This neglectful behavior causes a delay not just for the individual but also for the team and perhaps the division. This disparity in exception treatment is a regular occurrence in organizations.

Do not be discouraged when you encounter the inequitable application of rules across different individuals. Do not despise following the rules adopted by an organization. Seek to be legal and operate with integrity. God will take care of illegal behavior.

They may continue to ignore healthy partnerships with their team, but my integrity remains intact.

Who Stole Your Confidence?

We are bombarded with criticism, judgments, and fault finding, looking for the negative under the premise of working toward perfection, never hearing any positive feedback. We suffer beat down after verbal beat down, discouraged to the point of being afraid to try again. So many attacks on our psyche steal our confidence.

Our confidence has been taken drip by drip over painful moments throughout the years. We do not even know our fire left until one day, we no longer have the energy to lift our heads. Poor performance becomes good enough.

Sleep becomes our constant state and slumber our escape from an existence that denies we ever dared to dream or realize our visions. Why try when opposition comes from the very one who is appointed to lead me to my purpose? Why am I here?

The frustration and discouragement are overwhelming. Stop! Do not go! Stay here! You are not ready! In the very next breath, training causes me to go and do the work. But when I go, I am 'out of order' launching out on my own uncovered.

It appears more comfortable just to sit still and do nothing, but I am quickly reminded that being still is not equal to doing nothing.

It is not the same thing. I feel an internal pull and call to meet the needs of those in my community through community programs, building businesses that help people excel in their purpose and worship through song to change the atmosphere I have authority over. UGHH! Help me, Lord!

"Do not, therefore, fling away your fearless confidence, for it carries a great and glorious compensation of reward. For you have need of steadfast patience and endurance, so that you may perform and fully accomplish the will of God, and thus receive and carry away [and enjoy to the full] what is promised."

Hebrews 10:35-36 (AMPC)

When provided with instructions deep in your spirit to perform a task, it is in your best interest to respond positively, going forward with the actions required.

Here is something about when your soul is longing for you to take some action. Club Destiny, Inc is a non-profit that has been my baby for an exceptionally long time. It was my very first business entity.

We serve many young adults, kicking off their careers in the workplace as well as those navigating through college. As many of us know all too well, in every company, there are great leaders and weak leaders. There are great teams to work with and offensive units. There are fair decisions made and many wrong choices made.

Unfortunately, the realistic day-to-day blind spots in organizations are absent in schools. It is all on-the-job training. Club Destiny provides coaching to help others navigate workplace challenges and remain positive and creative in doing so.

A couple of years ago, I felt this urgency to start a new program in Club Destiny to assist young women in advancing and thriving in the workplace. I tried to ignore it; I did. But it only intensified and would not let me go.

Once I recognized that this work is my life's assignment, I finally gave in, and now we are assisting beautiful, thriving women.

I had to reconnect with my confidence that I could rebuild and restructure the organization and program. So, I assembled a team of women to support younger women.

The work we have done is needed. Not only are we helping the more youthful women we set out to help, but those of us who support them in leveling up is significantly better off because of this experience.

Negative situations occur to discourage us from having the confidence to reinvent what we tried before so we can meet the needs of those who are waiting for us to show up.

I showed up, and I was the only one in the room who looked like me. I am the only one in the room who understands what it is like to be a black woman, denied my authenticity of thoughts and tone of communication, and appearance.

My daily experience is in an environment that believes it is diverse. The truth is that I have been the only one in the room for the majority of my 40-plus-year career.

Occasionally, I had the pleasure of interacting with a black male or female in a different role. Often distance, capacity, or assignments prevented us from collaborating or working together. I am the only one in the room when conversations ensue, therefore having to choose my battles carefully.

Supporting the success of the organization is never a question because, after all, it is the right thing to do, and it contributes to my livelihood.

One must wonder, after all these years, if the company cannot find more qualified black people to join the organization. Are they not attracted to organizations where they do not see themselves at all levels of the organization? Is it possible that an organization's culture can be an enemy to its success goals?

Until I began to fully understand what I bring to the table and its value as a total package, my confidence was in jeopardy every day by off comments, lack of recognition, lack of promotion, and the diminishing of prime visible assignments.

I received the projects that no one else wanted, or no sponsor wanted for their protégé. I repeatedly deliver, with the teams alongside me, that leadership is amazed at the progress. It is a blessing.

Their comments indicate that they never thought we would be so successful. Who stole my confidence? What took my faith? Forty years of having to prove myself every day only to receive the opportunity to come in the next day and do it all over again.

Knowing that you are doing a great job but receiving no increases or bonuses will destroy your confidence if you are not aware of the root of your predicament.

Confidence comes from within and is reinforced or acknowledged externally. Have faith in your skills, your character, and your experiences.

There are times you must stand alone in your abilities to accomplish a task. No one will validate you. It is up to you to believe in you.

Your self-esteem is equally essential when someone attempts to define you by downgrading you in some capacity. Know who you are and who you are not so that you can stand confidently in the face of unwarranted and unproven opposition.

You define yourself through your past and by going forward. That is right; pursuing your strategy and goals fuels your confidence while establishing yourself deeper still. No one else will ever be able to do this for you.

Work It Until It No Longer Works for You

I pop my head up at 7:36 am in an instant of panic, thinking that I am running late only to realize that it is Saturday. Thank you, Lord, for Saturdays and Sundays. I lay there, still waiting for instruction. What do I need to do better? How can I get closer to where YOU (God) want me to be? I lay there in the still of the night and heard, "*Timing is critical. It will be a matter of saving your life or saving someone else's life.*" I never forgot that moment, and from that day forward, I had a great appreciation for the criticality of responding promptly.

On many occasions, I arrived to have a conversation that either changed their perspective or mine for the better. I arrived at the designated time only to receive the last item left that I needed for my next move. I had responded immediately to a request to reach out to someone in need and brought them to hope just when they were giving up hope.

Timing also involves knowing when to remain in a position or understanding the proper time to move on to a new job. Most of my cases have been to stay put much longer than I would have desired. Even when trying, I was unsuccessful in moving on when I tried to be at the helm of my career.

My experience is that I did not have to run from trouble or discomfort; it eventually left me. I just had to wait it out. I learned in the middle of my career that I was not there for myself as much as I was there to help others. Helping has proven to be true repeatedly ever since I was made aware of it. When I was in a position that was not ideal, I changed my focus to my real purpose for being in that position. My steps were orchestrated, and not even I could alter my path. It was not about me or for me. It was for someone else.

My advice to you is to be noticeably clear on your purpose and always be able to serve others and yourself. I am not convinced that it has to be one or the other. I believe in balance. The balance may come unexpectedly. You may find yourself creatively meeting your personal goals while still fulfilling your assignment to serve other individuals or an organization at large. The arrangement should, however, be mutually beneficial.

Perhaps helping your organization or individuals provides an experience you could not get elsewhere in a safe and secure environment with comfortability and ease. Maybe you will gain knowledge and skills that will be practical in the operation of your mission or service to a community for which you have a passion. No, it is not the ideal job for you, but it is a good fit because they have a similar vision. What better way to learn than being in an organization that is meeting the same need? I call this treading water. You are staying afloat by using just the right level of energy while building stamina as you develop a strategy for your next move.

When waiting for things to change, don't lose your confidence. Discouragement may set in and cause doubt in your value and worth. Build trust and maintain your confidence knowing that things are in motion even when they are not evident.

I recall sitting in a canoe during a youth leader's retreat, sharing with my canoe partner, Glenda, that I felt as though I was stuck and not moving forward because I was not driving hard to a finish line. I thought I was in a holding pattern. There was nothing I could do at this point. It was a time in my life when God was unwinding habits and mindsets that were not serving me well.

Many times, I wanted to help God by doing anything to speed up the process. It would not have been fruitful to do stuff just to be doing it. I had to wait for everything to align. I felt as though I was standing still. Sitting in that canoe, Glenda pointed out that we stopped rowing for quite some time as we were talking, yet we were not in the same spot we were in when the conversation began. She so eloquently pointed out that we were not doing anything, yet we were still moving. While it may appear as though I was standing still, I was not.

God had and still has everything under control, aligning the right scenarios and people to converge and the appointed intersection for continued success in my life. Glenda, my new friend, was correct. I never forgot the insight she shared. Often when I feel like I am not making the expected progress, I reflect on the lesson that I learned in that canoe on the lake.

Managing the Descent in the Organization Gracefully

Why would I seek coaching and mentoring now from someone who did not coach or mentor me when I was their direct report? Am I too far gone that this relationship is unsalvageable regardless of anyone's good intentions? Is it time to move on? In the meantime, I become 'me' focused and sponsored for my success.

No one else gets the credit for my journey in the traditional sense. There were more lessons of what not to do than there were about what to do. Unfortunately, even those from my community who were in a position to help did not, and perhaps they couldn't. They chose to provide cover that supported their journey. Was it their only option? I hear the chorus response, "*You should have gone after it as I did. Everyone has to make their way.*" In my solo response, I was not afforded the opportunity despite my reliable, competent performance in each assignment.

Some are the backbone of the organization, at least supported because they could be self-motivated with menial support. In essence, they are the ones fighting for their lives, for their very existence every day, all day. But by and through the grace of God, I would have gone crazy or died if He, the Holy Spirit, was not covering me, guiding me, protecting me, teaching me, and shaping me while others simply used me. Yes, I am "hired" to do a job, while others have the privilege of moving from being a hired hand to building a partnership that provides a service or product.

I want an organization that includes me as a valuable collaborative component in fulfilling its vision and mission. I will no longer simply be a means to an end. It does not feel good at any level of the organization. It does not feel good at all. But by the grace of God, I go into work past the growl of hell's hound dogs. I carry my hurt and disappointments, hidden or orderly, with solutions just waiting for the opportunity to safely express the wounds and trauma inflicted by those who should have had my best interest at heart.

Some who were responsible for the successful execution of my assignments through ongoing training, development, and coaching failed miserably. Instead, they stripped me of my confidence, dignity, and growth capacity through a lack of adequate and meaningful communication.

Better engagement would have caused the lifting of my head, soul, spirit, and in some cases, my body to be much more comfortable than it has been on this journey. It was not a journey of grace and ease as the privileged so often are allowed to experience without any effort.

And then, God says, "*You are there to help others.*" In all the daily fights I experienced, I am here to help others to survive the neglect, pain, and (in some cases) torture. But for the grace of God, there go I with a response of, "Yes, Lord."

Looking in the Face of Grace

On the surface, there appears to be an injustice. Perspective matters because, for me, that level of performance is acceptable.

Are the standards overall relaxed, or is there grace for some but not all? Have I walked into a higher grace realm? Am I receiving the same level of blessing or more magnificent blessing? Are we being tolerated versus celebrated? Is this the right place for me, or just a holding tank until something better comes along? When will better come?

I command better to go through my purpose and put myself in my place of destiny now because where I am now is not it. It is not the form and fulfillment I know is mine. I must walk in purpose now.

Or am I on a mission even in this holding pattern, this hovering position? When will my change come? I need divine change now so that I walk in my purpose all the days of my life. My latter is better, more significant!

Jackson and Ahmad were serving an organization in the same position. It was clear that Ahmad was valued by those he supported. He was trustworthy and credible. He was a person of color who struggled with colleagues who criticized his tone when participating in conversations and meetings.

Ahmad had to intentionally tailor his communication to avoid misinterpretation of being angry or judging, or uninviting. Ironically, his most senior leader, Kelsey, has outbursts in large meetings to the point of storming out of the room. Kelsey has been abrupt with those who reported to him, and observers were uncomfortable. However,

Ahmad must watch his tone when engaging in conversation in a routine meeting.

Trevor provided unreliable responses to those depending on his direction. He often did not remember what he said in a previous conversation or decision. At times, this caused rework and wasted valuable time as the demand for completed work was ever-increasing. An organizational change resulted in Ahmad, a Black man, getting demoted but maintaining some of his previous responsibilities and more detailed work for his new role.

Trevor, who is Caucasian, does not appear to add value nor deliver what is needed when needed remained in his position and was given great opportunities to join premier projects visible to the entire enterprise. Everyone only tolerates Trevor, yet they are happy to ignore his ineptness in supporting teams.

So, I asked God, *"What is going on here? How can this be tolerated?"* Honestly, it just did not seem fair. The response I received was, *"You are looking in the face of grace."*

Wow! Grace, the gift God chooses to give us when we do not deserve a gift at all. The unexplainable favor received when everything warrants just the opposite.

People are seeing something opposite or tolerating such poor performance when judgment would suggest dismissal. Thank you, God, for showing me the objective lesson of grace.

Leaders Have Bad Days and Stupid Moments

It is true. No one is perfect. It is hard at times to come with your 'A' game when the pressure becomes unbearable and the demand for more significant performance increases.

Life issues impact those you depend on for success, interrupting production flow. There are times when you just do not know what you are doing or how you will resolve the insurmountable items requiring your attention. The struggle is real.

I experienced Raymond, a senior leader's meltdown and tantrum all at once because he did not like what the team was conveying to him in a meeting. Raymond became physically angry, banging on the table and yelling demands at his direct reports in front of their staff.

I have heard church leaders randomly speaking from the pulpit and in meetings without considering the impact on others.

Everything, even when stated in context, can be damaging to individuals who are sensitive to the subject matter.

Constantly enhancing leadership and communication skills will reveal blind spots. The power of an apology from a leader does not diminish their influence. It enhances their impact, demonstrates humility, and offers an opportunity to increase credibility.

The key is not to continue to act in a way that requires constant apologies. The credibility factor, in those cases, becomes null and void.

Yes, leaders have bad days, but should it become a problem for their staff or even visible to the team? A bad day for a leader results in a drag on their group.

Is it worth it to leave personal concerns unresolved, costing the organization the very thing they are attempting to gain? I think not.

Leaders need self-care and confidants who can help them through the tough times to maintain momentum in setting direction.

Getting to a Secured Reality

The episodes of my life to date are not how I envisioned my career. I knew and heard about the glass ceiling plenty of times. I did not realize that it would eventually come crashing down on me. I defined it as a restriction to the heights of the elevation I could reach. I chose to maintain my values over advancing to a point where I would have to sacrifice my integrity and identity.

Little did I know that, along the way, the environment fought to deny my identity and desired assimilation. I never saw that the tug of war over my perseverance to stick and stay would cause the ceiling to lower upon me. Promotions, bonuses, and even standard increases at regular intervals had stopped. All of those were for the young valued employees who are potential flight risks.

When you reach retirement age showing evidence of building a life after this life, yet you are still here despite any chance for advancement, you are no longer a flight risk. You will stay until they do not know when, but it is not worth investing in monetarily. I attend a low-budget conference after convincing layers of management. The reality is that I need to stay until my assignment is up. Many years have passed since I became aware that this was not a job or career for me. Instead, it is an assignment to help those divinely assigned to me.

Watching this unfold over time, I reached a secured reality that as long as I took every job seriously, pouring all that I had into it, my personal needs are met. I lived it over and over again. I get great joy from helping others navigate through overwhelming, confusing, and unfair scenarios. Not that I would want anyone to have to go through these painful situations.

They are real and, too often, cause people to be unsuccessful. I am grateful. I share my experiences to empower others to move beyond being stuck or despondent. No one should have to experience hopelessness day in and day out when they are merely trying to make a decent living and have an opportunity to build a healthy, prosperous life for their families. It is what most people want.

On the outside, looking in, one would classify me as someone stuck. But I am not stuck. I am fulfilling a purpose that is working for my good and the good of others. I am in a secure reality as I wait to move to my best life. Although serving in this capacity allows me to benefit from my best existence, my best will get better.

The end is drawing near for this assignment. In the meantime, I choose to conduct myself at a high-level of performance. So, how do I conquer these corporate enemies?

I approach my day as a business owner on behalf of the company. I am building a conglomerate, and I am laying the foundation regarding how I want individuals who join my company to have the most exceptional integrity, innovation, creativity, passion, and compassion required to make my organization successful.

I continue to build meaningful relationships along the way. While the situation may not be the best, I am committed to being my best.

About the Author: Yvette C Owens

EXECUTIVE BIOGRAPHY

Yvette C Owens is a world-renowned speaker, international best-selling author, and leadership coach/consultant who teaches leaders the principles of change leadership to increase adoption, retain talent, and build high-performing teams using the proprietary V.I.C.T.O.R. framework.

The "Business Ambassador"

DestinySpeak Inc.
Helping Leaders Create Healthy Cultures Through Strategic Change

BOOKING CONTACT

Phone: +1 860 778 8524
Email: destinyspeakv2r@gmail.com
Website: destinyspeak.com
Location: Windsor, CT

SOCIAL MEDIA

Facebook: @DestinySpeakV2R
Twitter: @YvetteOwens1
Instagram: @destinyspeak
Store: @DestinySpeakInc
LinkedIn: @yvetteowensbusinessambassador

CORPORATE & BUSINESS

Yvette C Owens is a world-renowned speaker, international best-selling author, leadership coach, and consultant who teaches change leadership principles to increase adoption, retain talent, and build high-performing teams using the proprietary V.I.C.T.O.R. framework. Yvette, AKA Changologist, is a board-certified change management professional (A.C.M.P.). She has 40+ years of sharing her vibrant, resilience, compassion, and influence in teaching how to "Dealing With Resistance To Accept And Invest In Change" during keynote speeches and live and virtual working sessions.

PROFESSIONAL AFFILIATIONS
- CCMP Certified Change Management Professional
- SAFe Scaled Agile
- Certificate of Brand Ambassador-Lifetime Excellence
- Award International
- National Mentoring Program
- Connecticut Partnership Mentoring Program

MEDIA
- CNTV
- Centerpost Media Daily Show
- Hoinser Magazine World Book of Peace 2022
- International Women's Magazine, Hoinser Media
- Meticulous Moments Podcast
- Authors Millionaire Academy Broadcast
- The Douglas Coleman Show VE
- Hoinser Book Queens 2021
- And more…

SPEAKER HIGHLIGHTS

- Catalent Pharma Solutions
- SCORE Western Massachusetts
- CREC Schools
- Kingdom Business Academy
- Women Soar Summit
- Hartford Women's Leadership Summit
- The Kapptor Connection Conference
- Les Brown Online Sales Summit
- TAG Talks VIP Speaker
- Connected Leaders Academy
- And more…

CLIENTS

"You were totally awesome, Yvette Owens. Thank you for joining us and sharing your knowledge and insight." ~ Karen Lincoln, Catalent Pharma Solutions

---

"Yvette is an extremely competent professional with a track record of execution excellence. She is focused on enabling others to deliver as promised in a project leadership context and values getting to the root cause vs. being distracted by symptoms that can drain resources and add risks to scheduling. She is a dynamic speaker and creates a level of confidence amongst leadership that she is driving the effort toward success.

She is known to be a big-picture professional and wants to understand how she can deepen her tool set toward current or future assignments. The most recent example I am aware of is her desire to pursue the CCMP program/designation. She set a goal and maneuvered the organization such that she made it happen.

When I think of Yvette, the characteristics that immediately come to mind are Talented, Depth, Communicator, Smart, Capable and Thought Leader." ~Kevin Nicholson, Lean-N2-InsurTech

---

"Yvette is very knowledgeable in project management and professional development. On several occasions, Yvette customizes training for my team. She took the necessary time to understand my objectives and the needs of my team and over delivered. Yvette is at the top of my list for professional development consulting and project management. I highly recommend Yvette." ~ David Daye, Goodwin University

---

"Yvette takes great pride in her work. She cares about not only achieving the results but getting the desired result the right way with integrity, collaboration, and hard work." ~Mike McNally, Foremost A Farmers Insurance Company

---

"Yvette is a very detail-oriented project manager with exceptional skill at managing multiple deliverables at the same time. In addition to being a highly skilled project manager and staff manager, she is absolutely wonderful to work with. I would highly recommend Yvette for any project." ~ Matt Sweeney, ACE Group

---

"My memorable moment was, you are in control of your destiny. My takeaways are you are valuable, identify your gift and goals, and pursue your purpose." ~ Gwen Neal, Seat of Power Event Attendee

"Absolutely amazing...thank you so much! So important for morale." ~ LaVerne Littles, Company Culture with Yvette C Owens Podcast Listener

BOOK REVIEWS OF CONQUERING CORPORATE ENEMIES: MIND. PERSONALITIES. SITUATIONS.

"I read your book. It moved me. Thank you for putting yourself out there. I experienced several very similar scenarios that you described. Other scenarios you talked about I have not and have no words for. It's gross and such a shame, and I'm sorry it all happened to you. I am so inspired by you and how you have dealt with it all and in the ways that you are choosing to move forward. I want to support you and your endeavors tangibly." ~ Carolyn Theriault

"I saw your book on LinkedIn and downloaded it on Kindle. I read the entire thing in one day! Thank you for having the courage to write it and share your experiences and stories." ~ Erica Dougall

"You Nailed It! Addressing the issues of workplace discontent and challenges is not an easy topic. However, the author has done a great job of addressing these complicated situations." ~ Lady Diva T

"I wanted to thank you for paving the way for other African-Americans/West Indians. Your strength, intelligence, and perseverance have made you a great role model. I know I would not survive walking in your shoes. Thank you and continue being who you are because you are an inspiration. ~ Lisa Mair

www.ingramcontent.com/pod-product-compliance
Lightning Source LLC
Chambersburg PA
CBHW051002140626
46546CB00017B/2439